The Poetry
of Francisco Brines:
The Deconstructive Effects
of Language

The Poetry
of Francisco Brines:
The Deconstructive
Effects of Language

Judith Nantell

Lewisburg: Bucknell University Press
London and Toronto: Associated University Presses

Associated University Presses
440 Forsgate Drive
Cranbury, NJ 08512

Associated University Presses
25 Sicilian Avenue
London WC1A 2QH, England

Associated University Presses
P.O. Box 338, Port Credit
Mississauga, Ontario
Canada L5G 4L8

The paper used in this publication meets the requirements of the American National Standard for Permanence of Paper for Printed Library Materials Z39.48–1984.

Library of Congress Cataloging-in-Publication Data

Nantell, Judith.
    The poetry of Francisco Brines : the deconstructive effects of language / Judith Nantell.
            p.   cm.
    Includes bibliographical references and index.
    ISBN 0-8387-5277-2 (alk. paper)
    1. Brines, Francisco, 1932–   --Criticism and interpretation.
2. Postmodernism (Literature)   3. Time in literature.   4. Knowledge, Theory of, in literature.   5. Nothingness in literature.   I. Title.
PQ6652.R5Z78 1994
861'.64--dc20   93-30378
                                                                              CIP

For Chris, Maura, and Brigid, without whom
being would be insignificant.

Poetic writing is the most
advanced and refined mode
of deconstruction.
—Paul De Man

Contents

Abbreviations

AN   Francisco Brines, *Aún no* (Barcelona: Ocnos, 1971)

ED   Francisco Brines, *Poesía 1960–1977: Ensayo de una despedida* (Madrid: Visor, 1984)

IEL   Francisco Brines, *Insistencias en Luzbel* (Madrid: Visor, 1977)

LB   Francisco Brines, *Las brasas* (Madrid: Ediciones Rialp, 1960)

OR   Francisco Brines, *El otoño de las rosas* (Sevilla: Editorial Renacimiento, 1986)

PE   Francisco Brines, *Poemas excluidos* (Sevilla: Editorial Renacimiento, 1985)

PO   Francisco Brines, *Palabras a la oscuridad* (Madrid: Insula, 1966)

SP   Francisco Brines, *Selección propia* (Madrid: Cátedra, 1984)

CD   Barbara Johnson, *The Critical Difference. Essays in the Contemporary Rhetoric of Reading* (Baltimore and London: The Johns Hopkins University Press, 1980)

DCE   Joan Corominas and José A. Pascual, *Diccionario crítico etimológico castellano e hispánico* (Madrid: Gredos, 1980)

DIF   Jacques Derrida, "Différance," in *Margins of Philosophy* (Chicago: University of Chicago Press, 1982)

DLE   *Diccionario de la lengua española.* Real Academia Española. 19th ed. (Madrid: Espasa-Calpe, 1970)

H   *Harper's Latin Dictionary*, ed. E. A. Andrews (New York: American Book Co., 1907)

OED   *The Compact Edition of the Oxford English Dictionary* (Oxford: Oxford University Press, 1971, rpt. 1979)

OG   Jacques Derrida, *Of Grammatology*, translated by Gayatri Chakravorty Spivak (Baltimore: The Johns Hopkins University Press, 1976)

PD   Andrew P. Debicki, *Poetry of Discovery. The Spanish Generation of 1956–71* (Lexington: The University Press of Kentucky, 1982)

POS   Jacques Derrida, *Positions*, translated by Alan Bass (Chicago: The University of Chicago Press, 1981)

PU   Francisco Ribes, *Poesía última,* 3d ed. (Madrid: Taurus, 1975)

RD   G. Douglas Atkins, *Reading Deconstruction: Deconstructive Reading* (Lexington: The University Press of Kentucky, 1983)

RSP   Margaret H. Persin, *Recent Spanish Poetry and the Role of the Reader* (Lewisburg, Pa.: Bucknell University Press, 1987)

SSP   Jacques Derrida, "Structure, Sign, and Play in the Discourse of the Human Sciences," in *The Language of Criticism and the Sciences of Man: The Structuralist Controversy* edited by Richard Macksey and Eugenio Donato (Baltimore and London: The Johns Hopkins University Press, 1972)

Acknowledgments

My most grateful acknowledgment is to be given to Francisco Brines for graciously granting me permission to quote from his work. I am also thankful to *Editorial Renacimiento* for granting permission to draw on Brines's *El otoño de las rosas*. I am deeply indebted to Claudio Rodríguez and José Angel Valente for allowing me to cite their poems. I wish to thank Cristina Silver for granting permission to cite Rodríguez's "Alto jornal." I also wish to thank AMBIT Serveis Editorials for allowing me to cite Valente's "Primer poema." I also wish to acknowledge Indiana University Press for granting me permission to draw on Irene Harvey's *Derrida and the Economy of Différance*.

A shortened version of chapter 1, "The Quest(ioning) of Epistemological Ground: The Spanish Generation of 1956," appeared in *Studies in 20th Century Literature* 16, no. 1 (Winter 1992): 43–64, in a Special Issue on Contemporary Spanish Poetry, and is reprinted here by permission.

Preface

My work on Francisco Brines's poetry began a number of years ago, and many people assisted me along the way as I brought my research to book form.

I am especially grateful to Andrew P. Debicki who, for the last ten years, has kindly encouraged my ongoing work on Brines's poetry. I would like to extend heartfelt thanks to my current colleague and former Department Head, Charles Tatum, for affording me the time to complete the research for my book. My special thanks to the College of Humanities Faculty Research Mini-Grants Awards Committee of the University of Arizona, which graciously supported first the initial and then the final stages of my study. I would also like to acknowledge the Faculty Research Grant that I received from Florida State University in the summer of 1984 for an earlier study of Brines's poetry fundamental to my book.

A number of graduate students in the Department of Spanish and Portuguese at the University of Arizona played an important role in the development of my study. In the fall of 1991 I had the great pleasure of teaching a seminar on literary theory as applied to contemporary Spanish poetry. Portions of my book grew out of ideas discussed and refined during that seminar. I wish to acknowledge the students who participated in this dialogue: J. T. Abraham, Claudia Aburto-Guzmán, Joe Deters, John Dupuis, Dolores Durán-Cerda, Susan Fansler, Alicia Garza, Alfonso Illingworth, Michael Phillip Kristiansen, Ruth Román, and Patricia Voorhis. The indispensable research assistance of Cecil Steed and Jesús Romero Anaya is greatly appreciated. In addition, I wish to thank both Alfonso Illingworth and Jesús Romero Anaya for reviewing my translations of Spanish texts. Finally, Joe Deters deserves special thanks for his careful proofing of the manuscript, his many helpful suggestions, and his assistance in indexing.

This book could not have been written without a few very special people who helped me in important ways. I am especially grateful to my friend, Cecilia Yocupicio, for all that she has done for me. I wish to thank Lorenia Romero for helping me with the necessary correspondence. My parents, Jack and Ruth Nantell, and my sisters, Mary Nantell Pearce and Sharon Nantell, have never failed to offer encouragement, and to them I owe a great deal.

Lastly, I wish to acknowledge those dear to my heart. My daughters Maura and Brigid were infinitely patient as I worked on "Mama's book." Their respect for my research, genuine interest in my professional life, and interruptive and wonderfully spontaneous hugs, flower bouquets, and special drawings and paintings, often presented during my long hours before the computer screen, continually reinforced my commitment to be both a professor *and* a mother. The intellectual and personal support of Chris Maloney is substantial. Not only did my book profit greatly from our discussions but also it never could have been written without his significant and untiring efforts at having our family life run smoothly. His generosity and love know no bounds, and for both I am forever thankful. Finally, my muse, Watson, showed me, by living to the fullest his more than nine lives, that it was possible to face the finitude of being. I am grateful to them all.

The Poetry
of Francisco Brines:
The Deconstructive Effects
of Language

Introduction

It is because of *différance* that the movement of signification
is possible.   —Jacques Derrida

Reading proceeds by identifying and dismantling differences
by means of other differences that cannot be fully identified
or dismantled.   —Barbara Johnson

Francisco Brines's poetry of the last thirty years offers a sustained
inquiry into three significant philosophical themes, knowledge, the
present, temporal instant, and nonbeing, which his poetic voices repeatedly scrutinize in such collections as *Las brasas* (The embers), *Palabras
a la oscuridad* (Words to darkness), *Aún no* (Not yet), *Insistencias en
Luzbel* (Insistences on Lucifer), *Poemas excluidos* (Excluded poems),
Poemas a D. K. (Poems to D. K.), and *El otoño de las rosas* (The Autumn
of the roses).[1] This inquiry also entails a careful and, at times, painful
probing of what Brines metonymically refers to as the "desastre
metafísico del hombre" (metaphysical disaster of humankind) (*SP* 19)
forever constituting *and* dismantling human existence.[2] Throughout
Brines's poetry, his poetic speakers wrestle with such conflictual differences as knowledge perpetually oscillating with ignorance, the present moment unceasingly becoming past, and human existence endlessly displaying its own finitude.

  Born in 1932, Brines is one of the most important and influential
writers of the much acclaimed group of poets frequently named the
"Spanish Generation of 1956 –71," which includes Angel Crespo, Glo-
ria Fuertes, Jaime Gil de Biedma, Angel González, Manuel Mantero,
Claudio Rodríguez, Carlos Sahagún, and José Angel Valente, among
others. These poets share the common attitude that poetry *and* the act
of writing poetry are a means to knowledge, knowledge of human existence and human concerns. These poets, as Andrew Debicki points out

in *Poetry of Discovery. The Spanish Generation of 1956–71*, offer the
reader "the vision of poetry as a gradual act of knowledge" (*PD* 10),
and Margaret Persin, in *Recent Spanish Poetry and the Role of the Reader*, further stresses "Rather than viewing a poem as the end result, a pol-
ished museum piece," these poets "tend to offer their texts as merely
the starting point in the creative process. In producing the text, the poet
comes to know a facet of reality in a new way" (*RSP* 16).[3]

I began my study by examining the process of acquiring knowledge
by means of the poetic act in selected poems of Rodríguez, Valente and
Brines as I attempted to situate Francisco Brines's poetry within his
poetic grouping. While engaged in my investigation, however, I discovered that the poems under consideration offer differing views on the
(im)possibility of attaining knowledge by means of and with the assistance of writing the poetic text. The quest for knowledge manifested
in many works of the "Generation of 1956 –71" also involves, as we
shall see, a questioning not only of the nature of knowledge itself but
also of the language used to describe this quest. It is in this sense that
my study offers a reappraisal of the works of poets such as Rodríguez,
Valente, and especially Brines, my primary focus, and attempts to view
their poetry within the evolution of postmodernity in contemporary
Spain. My critical examination links Brines's poetry to postmodern
aesthetics and in so doing underscores the significance of his work
within the development of contemporary Western literature and current literary theory.

Looking specifically at chapter 1, I show that even though much of the
critical literature written about the poetry of the Spanish Generation
of 1956 –71 sustains that for the poets of this group writing poetry is a
means to knowledge, the concept of knowledge forever vacillates with
its apparent opposite, ignorance, whenever the supplement ruptures the
tidy arrangement of the knowledge/ignorance polarity.[4] It is thus no
longer possible to focus on either entity in isolation. While examining
"Alto jornal" (Superior day-wages) of Claudio Rodríguez, "Primer
poema" (First poem) of José Angel Valente, and "Esplendor negro"
(Black splendor) of Francisco Brines, I explore poetry *not* as a process
of knowing but rather as a method for questioning epistemological
ground. Both the poetic text and the interpretive text present knowledge and ignorance forever becoming their own *différance*.[5]

Throughout each of Brines's poetic collections we witness the asking of various metaphysically framed questions in the form of "What
is . . . ?" Chapter 2 discusses a query fundamental to Brines's poetry:
"What is time?" This question appears to be one that requests or
requires a definition; yet, as we shall see, no singular, straightforward,

precise definition is ever forthcoming in Brines's poetry. Rather, the critic repeatedly encounters various poetic speakers recounting the knotted problems of human existence entangled within "el tejido del tiempo" (the weave of time) (*ED* 157) that is Brines's poetry.

How could the critic enter this textual-temporal-existential "weave"? In chapter 2 I test two critical strategies, each of which allows a possible point of entrance. First, I attempt to disentangle the numerous thematic fibers in the interwoven, temporal texts of Brines's poetry. In the first part of this chapter my ordering, sorting, unraveling of the various thematic strands demonstrate the futility of this undertaking. This attempted disentwining reveals instead that no singular, temporal, thematic thread can be isolated successfully, namely because each remains inextricably bound to the textual tangle of the Brinesean "weave of time." I then shift my attention to interrogating the question "What is time?" and my interrogation leads to other questions in the supplementary series of questions concerning time repeatedly asked by various poetic speakers in Brines's poetry: "What is the present?" "What is the present instant?" "What is the conscious present?" My second critical strategy involves scrutinizing the interlaced strands constituting the center of Brines's textual, temporal "weave": the present moment. Because human being[6] exists *within* what Brines terms, "el fragilísimo presente" (the very fragile present) (*SP* 41), the entire woven fabric of human existence is flimsy, delicate, weak and thus subject to unraveling each time the personal, present instant comes into existence *and* ceases to be. My interrogation of poems such as "Un olor de azahar" (A fragrance of citrus blossoms), "Elca," "Elca y Montgó" (Elca and Montgó), and "Lamento en Elca" (Lament in Elca) shows that each poem constitutes a different version of human being's acute awareness of the present moment ceaselessly becoming past.

The analysis of nonbeing, a constant theme in Brines's poetry, is the subject of chapter 3, where I explore yet another significant question often asked by many Brinesean voices: "What is 'la nada'?" (nothingness). Focusing on the poet's act of naming "la nada," I examine multiple efforts on the part of various poetic speakers to define and redefine, present and re-present this ontological concept. At first, the critic might believe that such persistent attempts ultimately will lead poet, speaker and, finally, critic to a singular, unequivocal, determinate naming. Such a naming would reduce all differences, ultimately leading the poet, his poetry, and the critic, to mastery of the concept named, the act of naming, and the language used in naming. Careful examination of Brines's poetry, however, reveals that the poet's activity of naming and renaming leads not to a singular naming but rather to a multiplicity of names, a multiplicity of differing designations. In poems such as "Definición de la nada" (Definition of nothingness), "Física de la muerte" (Physical death), "Tríptico de la aventura" (Triptych of the adventure), "Las últimas preguntas" (The final questions), and "El encuentro" (The meeting), to mention only a few, the concept of "la nada" is not reduced to a singular essence that is always the same, a singular essence designated and defined always in the same way, always by the same name. Rather, this ontological concept is expanded, enlarged, extended by the movement of *différance* playfully at work within the act of naming.

During the course of writing the three chapters central to my study of Brines's poetry, little by little I came to see that the asking of the metaphysically framed questions "What is knowledge?", "What is time?", and "What is nonbeing?" carried with it the very condition for both the possibility and the impossibility of arriving at a determinate answer. My own critical interrogation of Brines's poetic interrogation is a quest that is, in essence, a constant questioning of knowledge, of the present instant, and of nonbeing, a quest that is a constant questioning of the various queries and answers produced and coerced by both the poetic and interpretive texts.

In the various readings of Francisco Brines's poetry offered in my study, I carefully examine "the working forces of signification that would conceal the play of difference" showing, as Danny Anderson so aptly puts it, "such differences constitute the very basis of signification" (149). My analyses concern assiduous scrutiny of the deconstructive effects of language, of language struggling with and against itself, of textual discontinuities, of the irreconcilable, semantic differences colluding and colliding with one another within the medium utilized by poet and critic alike. My interrogation, both of the poem and the interpretive readings of the poem, leads to a critique of the textual contradictions and aberrations that subvert fixed meaning whenever the difference that is textuality keeps language in play. My critical study, thus, both adheres to and promotes the critical strategy of crossexamining language which, as Jacques Derrida has shown us, always already "bears within itself the necessity of its own critique"(*SSP* 254).[7]

Deconstruction, by foregrounding interrogation, places questioning at the center of the critical enterprise. As G. Douglas Atkins explains:

> To ask a question of a text is an attempt to coerce a response; it is an attempt to make the "respondent" willing to answer. But the response from the text, which is also will-ing, is incomplete at best, and that serves merely to create additional questions. Imposition thus occurs, and it comes from both critic and text. What emerges is a battle of wills between text and critic—a dialogue

of questions that is mutual coercion. Mutually dependent on language, critic and text question each other, read each other. They are thus caught in an inevitable and ceaseless oscillation in which neither text nor critic dominates, acts as master to the slave-other. (*RD* 87–88)

The emphasis in my various interpretive readings of Brines's poetry is on the act of critical interrogation and not on the formulation of definitive answers to the numerous queries asked. As we shall often see throughout the course of my critical study, the answers offered in both the poetic *and* the interpretive texts are numerous, often contradictory, and stubbornly heterogeneous. My critical interpretation of Francisco Brines's poetry has not led to precise, exact, interpretive discourse clarifying, once and for all, the poem's discourse. Rather, both Brines's poems and my critical readings of his poems constitute different versions of the "conflictuality of *différance*" (*POS* 44) forever at play *within* written discourse.

My critical study, like the poetry examined therein, offers a way both to look at and live through the problems encountered whenever we grapple with meaning, knowing, and nonbeing within the ephemeral present moment in which the act of writing about such concerns takes place. I attempt not to resolve these problems but rather to engage in an ongoing and never-ending questioning. I also attempt not to reduce but rather to open the text, both poetic and critical, by means of the process of interrogation. Both Brines's poetry and my critical commentary on his poetry provide the reader with a way to begin to discuss not only existential concerns but also to learn what is involved when poet and critic attempt to name, to address, to comment on, and to interpret these concerns in written language ceaselessly engaged in a semantic struggle with itself.

Francisco Brines's poetry has not been translated into English. It is thus fitting in this introduction to my study of his poetry that I close with a word regarding presenting works to an audience that more than likely will be familiar with both Spanish and English. In my critical interpretations and my translations of Brines's poetic texts I attempt to consider carefully "the play of differences within language" (*DIF* 15). This "play of differences" is highlighted dramatically when one attempts to translate: "to turn from one language into another" (*OED* 3381). My differing and often deferring substitutions express inexactly, imprecisely, and in other words the words of Brines's poems. It is this act of translating, however, that has led me to follow, in yet another way, the twists, turns, and movement of *différance*.

1
Questioning Epistemological Ground

Si fallor, sum   —St. Augustine

What is known remains inexact, what is mastered insecure.
                                                 —Martin Heidegger

Much of the critical literature written about the poetry of what has frequently been called the "Generation of 1956 –71" sustains that for
Claudio Rodríguez, José Angel Valente, and Francisco Brines, among
other members of this group, writing poetry is a means to knowledge.
The various *poéticas* written by many of these poets, especially during
the 1960s, corroborate and advance this fundamental view. Andrew
Debicki explains that in this generation we find the stress has been
placed on poetry as "an act of discovery and knowledge rather than
mere communication" (*PD* 7). Margaret Persin later observes: "Vir-
tually all of the poets of this generation view the act of writing as their
best method of knowing reality" (*RSP* 22). Carole Bradford elaborates
in "The Dialectic of Nothingness in the Poetry of Francisco Brines":
"For the majority of the poets of the second post-war group, art is a
means to knowledge . . ." (1).

For poets such as Valente, the process of poetry *is* the process of
knowledge, evident in his "Poética" published in 1966 in Antonio Molina's *Poesía española contemporánea* (Contemporary Spanish poetry):
"Escribo poesía porque el acto poético me ofrece una vía de acceso,
para mí insustituible, a la realidad. Quizá no es difícil desprender de
ahí que veo la poesía en primer término como conocimiento y sólo en
segundo lugar como comunicación" (I write poetry because the poetic
act offers me a via of access, which for me cannot be substituted, to reality. Perhaps it is not difficult to deduce that I see poetry primarily as
knowledge and only secondly as communication) (Molina 489).
Rodríguez explains his view of poetry and cognition in this way in

8

"Unas notas sobre poesía" published in Francisco Ribes's anthology *Poesía última* (Latest poetry): "El proceso del conocimiento poético es el proceso mismo del poema que lo integra" (The process of poetic knowledge is the same process as that of the poem that integrates it) (*PU* 87). Finally, Brines affirms that by writing poetry "el poeta trata de conocer, de indagar una oculta verdad" (the poet tries to know, to inquire into a hidden truth) (Molina 528).[1]

Since knowledge, however, vacillates with its apparent opposite, ignorance, and because the trace assures that these dichotomies forever will be linked, forever will be accomplices of each other, forever will be undermined by each other, it is not possible to focus on knowledge in isolation.[2] Neither knowledge nor ignorance can have meaning without the other. As Atkins points out, since the trace keeps "language forever in play" and insures "the perpetual oscillation of meanings" it thus deconstructs "our usual way of thinking in simple oppositions" (*RD* 81). When scrutinizing selected poems of Rodríguez, Valente, and Brines, we shall discover that poetry is not a process of knowing but rather it is a process of questioning the grounds of knowledge.

As critics we must rethink the concept of knowledge in textual terms. When we do, Valente's famous dictum, "todo poema es un conocimiento haciéndose" (every poem is knowledge becoming) (*PU* 158), which long has served as the foundation of both the poetry of this generation and the critical literature written about this poetry, itself is reconstituted in terms of ignorance.[3] If knowledge and ignorance continually interimplicate each other, then Valente's assertion at once underscores *and* undermines the privileged term in the hierarchical opposition knowledge/ignorance because, as we shall learn, "todo poema es un conocimiento haciéndose" (every poem is knowledge becoming) its own *différance*.[4]

In each of the poems studied here, the poet tries to master knowledge through language. This mastery, however, is subverted by the "warring forces of signification," to borrow Barbara Johnson's observation ("Introduction" xiv), and what is known remains inexact. In Rodríguez's "Alto jornal" (Superior day-wages), the literal reading of a key phrase unravels the figural reading as the poem's protagonist arrives at (in)sufficient knowledge. The "conflictuality of *différance*" (*POS* 44) inherent in language undermines the protagonist's mastery of "el canto" (the song) in Valente's "Primer poema" (First poem). Finally, the shadow presence of the "Esplendor negro" (Black splendor), which is also the title of Brines's poem, subverts the process of coming to know examined in the text. Brines's poetry exemplifies yet one other differing view on Valente's adage. Writing poetry, as the deconstructive reading of "Esplendor negro" will demonstrate, is *not* a process of knowing but rather it is a process of questioning ceaselessly epistemological ground.[5]

A passage from Rodríguez's "Unas notas sobre poesía" (Some notes on poetry) summarizes clearly this poet's view of poetry as an act of knowing: "Creo que la poesía es, sobre todo, participación. Nace de una participación que el poeta establece entre las cosas y su experiencia poética de ellas, a través del lenguaje. Esta participación es un modo peculiar de conocer" (I believe that poetry is, above all, participation. It is born from a participation that the poet establishes between things and his poetic experience of them, through language. This participation is a peculiar form of knowing) (*PU* 87). This cognitive "participation" is the underlying theme of Rodríguez's "Alto jornal" (Superior day-wages) (*Desde mis poemas* 97), first published in 1958 in *Conjuros* (Conjurations).[6]

> Dichoso el que un buen día sale humilde
> y se va por la calle, como tantos
> días más de su vida, y no lo espera
> y, de pronto, ¿qué es esto?, mira a lo alto
> y ve, pone el oído al mundo y oye,   5
> anda, y siente subirle entre los pasos
> el amor de la tierra, y sigue, y abre
> su taller verdadero, y en sus manos
> brilla limpio su oficio, y nos lo entrega
> de corazón, porque ama, y va al trabajo   10
> temblando como un niño que comulga
> mas sin caber en el pellejo, y cuando
> se ha dado cuenta al fin de lo sencillo
> que ha sido todo, ya el jornal ganado,
> vuelve a su casa, alegre y siente que alguien   15
> empuña su aldabón, y no es en vano.

> One day the fortunate man humbly departs
> and goes down the street, like so many
> other days of his life, and he doesn't expect it
> and, suddenly, what is this?, he looks up at the sky
> and sees, he puts his ear to the world and listens,   5
> he walks, and he feels rising from among his footsteps
> the love of the earth, and he goes on, and he opens
> his genuine workshop, and in his hands
> his occupation shines brightly, and he hands it over to us
> sincerely, because he loves, and he goes to work   10
> trembling like a child receiving communion

but without getting fat, and when
he has realized finally how simple
it has all been, now his day-wages earned,
he returns to his house, happy and he senses that someone   15
grasps his door knocker, and it is not in vain.

The poem records a day in the life of the workman-protagonist. His active and enthusiastic participation in his everyday world leads to what could be described as a reverent understanding not only of this world (lines 5–7) but also of the next, as the poem's title and final lines suggest. As a single, extended sentence, divided into hendecasyllabic verses with assonantal monorhyme of *a–o* in the even numbered verses, the poem records the rhythmical footsteps (line 6) of the workman as he departs from his home, arrives at his workshop, and returns home again. Anaphorically linked throughout the poem, many of the protagonist's actions reinforce the measured, repeated, two syllable verbal pattern echoing the cadence of his journey: "sale, se va, mira, pone, oye, anda, sigue, abre, ama, vuelve" (departs, goes, looks, puts, listens, walks, continues, opens, loves, returns) (lines 1–15). On this particular day, however, something out of the ordinary occurs (lines 4 –13). The protagonist discovers the deep-seated meaning of his daily existence:

> . . .y abre
> su taller verdadero, en sus manos
> brilla limpio su oficio, y nos lo entrega
> de corazón   (lines 7–10)

> . . . and he opens
> his genuine workshop, in his hands
> his occupation shines brightly, and he hands it over to us
> sincerely

His work, as humble as it may be, is of value, he comes to learn, because it is done for others. The emphasis is thus placed on the positive act of discovery and the positive value of the protagonist's "oficio," that is, the "service" he performs for others, as the Latin source, *officium*, underscores (*H* 1260).

The revelatory, illuminative experience of comprehending "lo sencillo que ha sido todo" (how simple it has all been) (lines 13–14) is the protagonist's figurative remuneration, "el jornal ganado" (the earned day-wages) (line 14). This reward, originating in and resulting from his daily work, serves as a metaphor for the workman's future "Alto jornal" (Superior day-wages) alluded to in lines 4–5 and lines 14–16, and conveyed in the poem's title. As Debicki observes, "In "Alto jornal" a workman's salary is presented both representationally and as a sign for life's meaning" (*PD* 49).[7] The protagonist's cognitive participation in his daily work, which cannot be separated from his daily life, leads to a profound understanding both of his present and future "alto jornal" and his present and future *jornada* (working day, journey). The workman's daily trip to his workshop serves as a metaphor for both his passage through life here on this earth and his future passage from this life to the next. The verb "comulga" (line 11), further stresses not only the protagonist's active participation in his daily life and the union he has achieved with his community of clients (lines 8–11), but also the revered importance of the series of events that have taken place on this extraordinary day, events culminating in Rodríguez's own sharing with others of knowledge acquired during the poetic process.[8]

Rodríguez describes this act of coming to know in both sacred, as it were, and profane terms: "y va al trabajo / temblando como un niño que comulga / mas sin caber en el pellejo"(he goes to work / trembling like a child receiving communion / but without getting fat) (lines 10–12). The underlying colloquial phrase, "no caber uno en el pellejo," carries the figurative meaning "to be very fat, to be very proud" (*DLE* 1000). In the poem, this revised common phrase, expressed in the everyday terms of a workman, quietly calls attention to both the vast amount of knowledge gained and the protagonist's complete satisfaction in gaining it. In the context of the poem, the use of the colloquial expression is at once humorous, especially if we consider the size of the host metaphorically alluded to in line 10, and revealing. The poet's demythification of *comulga* by means of everyday language, underscores the process of acquiring knowledge of, first, everyday life and, later, eternal life: "se ha dado cuenta al fin de lo sencillo / que ha sido todo" (he has realized finally how simple / it has all been) (lines 13–14). When the underlying idiomatic expression in question is used with the function word *no*, which expresses the negative of an alternative possibility, then what is conveyed is that, literally, the person involved does not fit into his skin anymore because, figuratively, he is getting so fat that his skin is bursting and no longer fits him. Or, if pride is involved, he is so filled with pride that he no longer fits into his own skin. Or, if knowledge is involved, as it is in the Rodríguez poem, then the protagonist is, thus, more than satisfied with the discovery that was made and the resultant understanding gained.

If we scrutinize the idiom, however, we see that it is introduced by the adversative conjunction *mas* (but), a connective that "joins" two dissimilar, opposing, different propositions. *Mas* is also an anomoly because in almost every line of the poem preference is given to the coordinating conjunction *y* (and), repeated fourteen times. Difference is signaled immediately, however, not only because of the presence of *mas* but also due to the poet's liberal substitution of *sin* (without) for *no* in the now revised, idiomatic expression, "sin caber en el pellejo" (line 12). *Sin* denotes absence or want, thereby adding to the colloquial idiom the notion of lack that it does not have with the underlying presence of the function word *no* in the expression "no caber en el pellejo." Looking at the altered idiom and its appearance in the text, we see that it is not the case that the protagonist no longer fits into his skin after "ingesting," figuratively speaking, knowledge of the meaning of his existence, but rather that he "ingests" this knowledge without fitting into his skin, perhaps because he has taken in too much, or perhaps because he has taken in not quite enough and, thus, there is still more room, more capacity.

It turns out that the grounds of the first reading of the text are ungrounded when the critic pursues the duplicitous nature of the altered idiomatic expression "sin caber en el pellejo" (line 12). Both the expression itself and its alteration call attention to the work of the supplement. *Sin* not only replaces *no* but also adds to the idiom, as well as to the theme of sufficient knowledge of the first reading, the notion of absence thus foregrounding the possibility of insufficient knowledge. Perhaps, then, it is because the workman-protagonist is (in)sufficiently satisfied that he both seeks and accepts the "alto jornal" of the poem's final lines. The holding of, the capacity for, the comprehending of the meaning of daily existence, of the first reading, are undermined by the second reading when the notion of absence, marked by *sin,* comes into play.[9]

Additionally, we face in the word *pellejo*, in the idiom of which it is part, and in the text as a whole, what Barbara Johnson calls "the proliferation of plays of the signifier" (Introduction xxix). If *pellejo* originally conveyed the meaning of a small skin or hide then literally reading line 12, some object (concept) might not "fit into" it because the skin itself is too small.[10] If that is the case, then, the revised idiom, as it appears and functions in the poem, points to not only the possibility of insufficient knowledge attained but also, and importantly, the added possibility that the container, the synecdochic skin-body and/or the mind-receptacle of the seeker of knowledge, is simply too small to hold what is learned and what is known will never be comprehended fully. The figural reading advanced in the first reading of particularly lines 10–14, and of the text in general, is subverted and reconstructed in terms of the literal reading of the altered idiomatic expression advanced in the second reading. It is the literal reading of the revised idiom that leads to not "lo sencillo / que ha sido todo" (how simple / it has all been) (lines 13–14), as the text asserts and the first reading of the poem advances, but rather widespread and duplicitous complications of expression and meaning engendered by the direct confrontation of the figural and literal levels of language and, consequently, the warring, thematic forces of sufficient knowledge *and* insufficient knowledge.[11]

José Angel Valente, like many of the other poets of his generation, regards the poem as a "progressive act of discovery" (*PD* 103) where the poet continually attempts to master knowledge by means of language within the poetic process. "Primer poema" (First poem), first published in *Poemas a Lázaro* (1960) (Poems to Lazarus), affirms his view of poetry: "el proceso de la creación poética sea un movimiento de indagación y tanteo en el que la identificación de cada nuevo elemento modifica a los demás o los elimina porque todo poema es un conocimiento haciéndose" (the process of poetic creation is a movement of inquiry and approximation in which the identification of each new element modifies all the others or eliminates them because every poem is knowledge becoming) (*PU* 157–58). Valente considers poetry as a means to knowledge and for him, and others of his group, knowledge cannot be separated from nor understood without inquiry. As such, his poetry displays a systematic investigation into his own various attempts at poetic creation, viewed repeatedly as "un movimiento de indagación y tanteo."[12] This is especially evident in "Primer poema" (*Punto cero* 61–62) where the act of writing is first described as one of combat and the poem's speaker, who could be viewed as a poet-writer, first sees himself in constant conflict with and questioning his medium:

> No debo
> proclamar así mi dolor.
> Estoy alegre o triste y ¿qué importa?
> ¿a quién ayudaré?
> ¿qué salavación podré engendrar con un lamento?   5
>
> Y, sin embargo, cuento mi historia,
> recaigo sobre mí, culpable
> de las mismas palabras que combato.
>
> Paso a paso me adentro,
> preciosamente me examino,   10
> uno a uno lamento mis cuidados
> ¿para quién,

qué pecho triste consolaré,
qué ídolo caerá,
que átomo del mundo moveré con justicia?   15
Remotamente quejumbroso,
remotamente aquejado de fútiles pesares,
poeta en el más venenoso sentido,
poeta con la palabra terminada en un cero
odiosamente inútil,   20
cuento los caedizos latidos
de mi corazón y ¿qué importa?
¿qué sed o qué agobiante
vacío llenaré de un vacío más fiero?

Poeta, oh no,   25
sujeto de una vieja impudicia:
mi historia debe ser olvidada,
mezclada en la suma total
que hará la verdadera.
Para vivir así,   30
para ser así anónimamente
reavivada y cambiada,
para que el canto, al fin,
libre de la aquejada
mano, sea sólo poder,   35
poder que brote puro
como un gallo en la noche,
como en la noche, súbito,
un gallo rompe a ciegas
el escuadrón compacto de las sombras.   40

I should not
proclaim my pain this way.
I am happy or sad and what does it matter?
Whom will I help?
What salvation will I be able to engender with a lament?   5

And, however, I tell my story
I fall back on myself, blameworthy
of the very words that I combat.

Step by step I move inward,
preciously I examine myself,   10
one by one I lament my concerns
For whom,
what sad breast will I console,

what idol will fall,
what worldly atom will I move with justice?   15
Confusedly complaining,
confusedly afflicted with futile sorrows,
poet in the most venomous sense,
poet with the word terminated in a zero
hatefully useless,   20
I count the fading beats
of my heart and what does it matter?
What thirst or what oppressed
void will I fill with a more ferocious void?

Poet, oh no,   25
the subject of an old shamelessness:
my story should be forgotten,
mixed with the total sum
that will make the true one.
To live this way,   30
to be anonymously
re-enlivened and changed,
so that the song, at last,
free of the afflicted
hand, may be only power,   35
pure power that springs forth
as a rooster in the night,
as in the night unexpectedly,
a rooster blindly breaks apart
the dense squadron of shadows.   40

The speaker's struggle, however, is not merely with his medium. It is also with his subject, or more precisely, self as subject. "Primer poema" demonstrates the speaker's dissentive views on writing self-indulgent poetry that directly, effusively and without any sense of modesty proclaims the intimate, emotional state of the poet (lines 1–24). The speaker's opening assertion, "No debo / proclamar así mi dolor" (I should not / proclaim my pain this way) (lines 1–2), is itself a critique of poetry solely concerned with expressing "los caedizos latidos / de mi corazón" (fading beats / of my heart) (lines 21–22). The writer of such verse is described as "remotamente quejumbroso, / remotamente aquejado de fútiles pesares / poeta en el más venenoso sentido" (confusedly complaining, / confusedly afflicted with futile sorrows / poet in the most venomous sense) (lines 16 –18).

Lines 25– 40 of the poem, however, stand in direct opposition to the critique of poet as subject developed in lines 1–24 of the opening section. In the final sixteen lines of "Primer poema" the protagonist searches for and finally encounters a new poet, a new subject matter, and a new poem: a poet who is no longer "sujeto de una vieja impudicia" (the subject of an old shamelessness) (line 26), a subject matter where "mi historia debe ser olvidada, / mezclada en la suma total / que hará la verdadera" (my story should be forgotten, / mixed with the total sum / that will make the true one) (lines 27–29), and a poem conceived as an illuminative "canto . . . poder que brote puro" (song . . . pure power that springs forth) (lines 33, 36).

Valente's "Primer poema" is about friction: poet struggling with his medium, poet struggling with and against his subject matter, poet struggling with the purpose of writing: "¿qué importa? / ¿a quién ayudaré? / ¿qué salvación podré engendrar con un lamento?" (What does it matter? / Whom will I help? / What salvation will I be able to engender with a lament?) (lines 3–5). The device of the rhetorical question, used frequently in the first part of the poem (lines 3, 4, 5, 12–15, 22, 23–24), serves to underscore both the protagonist's frustration and skepticism in expressing and questioning why he writes: "cuento los caedizos latidos / de mi corazón y ¿qué importa?" (I count the fading beats / of my heart and what does it matter?) (lines 21–22). The tripartite conflict of the poem's first twenty-four lines culminates in lines 19–20 when the speaker characterizes the subject ("poeta"), the medium ("palabra"), and the purpose ("terminada en un cero") of his writing as "odiosamente inútil": "poeta con la palabra terminada en un cero / odiosamente inútil" (poet with the word terminated in a zero / hatefully useless). Such nihilism and nullity lead to the final rhetorical question of the first part of "Primer poema": "¿qué sed o qué agobiante / vacío llenaré de un vacío más fiero?" (What thirst or oppressed / void will I fill with a more ferocious void?) (lines 23–24).

"Primer poema" is a clear manifestation of a poem that is, to use Valente's own words, "un conocimiento haciéndose" (knowledge becoming) (*PU* 158). The poem, as we have seen, is about discord but discord that is becoming accord. The "poeta con la palabra terminada en un cero" (line 19) of the first moment now comprehends, in the second moment, that "mi historia debe ser olvidada, / mezclada en la suma total / que hará la verdadera" (my story should be forgotten, / mixed with the total sum / that will make the true one) (lines 27–29). Only after poet as subject has been transformed into "suma total . . . reavivada y cambiada" (total sum . . . re-enlivened and changed) (lines 28, 32) can the new poem- "canto" emerge. Thus, in this poem, the struggle is not merely for mastery of word and mastery of subject but also for knowledge, specifically, mastery of knowledge through the process of poetic creation. Ultimately, the speaker-protagonist of "Primer poema" comes to learn:

> ... el canto, al fin,
> libre de la aquejada
> mano, sea sólo poder,
> poder que brote puro
> como un gallo en la noche,
> como en la noche, súbito,
> un gallo rompe a ciegas
> el escuadrón compacto de las sombras.   (lines 33–40)

> ... the song, at last,
> free of the afflicted
> hand, may be only power,
> pure power that springs forth
> as a rooster in the night,
> as in the night unexpectedly,
> a rooster blindly breaks apart
> the dense squadron of shadows.

Here, rhetorical questions have been replaced by answers that are, in themselves, affirmations of the positive resolution of conflict. If the opening lines of the poem's final moment (lines 25–26) are viewed as apostrophic, then, as the etymological overtones of "apostrophe" convey, and as the emphatic interjection "oh no" further sustains, the speaker-protagonist "turns away" from the type of poet and poetry described in lines 1–24. Armed with knowledge, he is now free to write about the new poet and the new poetry characterized in lines 25–40.

When the final lines of "Primer poema" are interrogated the critic finds that all along the speaker's struggle has been with ignorance. What is discovered, as the poem develops, is that ignorance will be vanquished by means of the illuminative "song," which is, in Valente's poetry, "un conocimiento haciéndose" (knowledge becoming). The poet underscores the elucidating potential of the poem-song with the metaphor of the vigilant rooster of dawn that vociferously greets the sun of illumination. Persin puts it this way: "the poet must resort to metaphor in order to describe the momentary success of 'el canto'. It is the unexpected suggestion of light—'un gallo en la noche'—that is able to break, if only fleetingly, 'el escuadrón compacto de las sombras'" (*RSP* 30).[13]

The metaphor of the rooster, thus, figures prominently in the first reading of the poem. The entire scheme established by the first reading, however, is undermined in terms of a second reading when the duplicitous semantic effects of the figure "un gallo en la noche" (a rooster in the night) are allowed to come into play. The text asserts the liberation of the "song" in lines 33–35, as we have seen, proclaiming the authoritative independence of the product of poetic creation. The mastery of the word, however, is only momentary (lines 33–37). Despite the poet-speaker's claim that the poem is free from the synec-dochic "hand" (line 34) of its writer and despite the additional claim that the resulting "song" is "pure power that springs forth" (line 36), the simile "como un gallo" (like a rooster) can call for another, this time divergent, interpretation to the one advanced in the first reading.

The mastery of the song seems to rest not with the song itself, as the text asserts, but rather with its composer and singer, for the ubiq-uitous presence of the poet-singer underlies the figure "un gallo en la noche." As the composer of "el canto," the poet-speaker metonym-ically assumes the dominant, valiant, authoritative role of the bird of dawn and therefore is viewed as master not only of the poem-song but also of the illuminative word that ultimately conquers ignorance. The poet-speaker, who at first struggled both with his medium and sub-ject matter, emerges victorious in the poem's final lines 36 – 40, and the repercussions of his underlying presence are felt in each sound of the figural cock's crow. It is the vigilant poet-"gallo" who greets the day with and by means of his song thereby reclaiming his place as master of both song and knowledge. In his role as master he thus usurps the potential originally attributed to "el canto" (lines 35–36).

The poem, however, also functions against its own assertions in yet another way. It is not the poet who combats language, as is claimed (line 8). Rather, it is language that is combative chiefly because, as deconstructive reading shows, language is the play of conflictive dif-ferences. This conflict manifests itself, to use one example, when the noun "gallo" is interrogated. In Spanish, as we know, *gallo* denotes a rooster, a cock. The word, however, also carries the familiar and figu-rative connotation of a false note that occurs inadvertently in song, speech, or while declaiming (*DLE* 651). A dissonant and openly com-bative interpretation now arises when the poet-singer and poem-song, the metaphoric rooster and illuminative cock-crow of the first reading, are viewed "differently." If the "double-edged word" (Johnson, "Intro-duction" xiv) "gallo" of the final lines, is read as "false note" or "sour note" then the poem-song is not "pure power that springs forth," as the text asserts in line 36. The twists and turns of language take us to a dis-crepancy: the song is weakened by the sour note that is sung, even if sung unintentionally or unexpectedly (line 38). The duplicitous "gallo" of both the poet-speaker's act of singing and of the resultant song undermines the metaphoric "power" of the poetic composition. The inscribed other message, at once caught up in and constituting the combative forces of signification, takes both poet and critic through the detours of language. Mastery of knowledge by means of language always already is subverted by the differing and deferring nature of language itself.[14]

In the works of many of the poets of the Generation of 1956 –71 as we have seen, we witness the complicity of writing and coming to know. It is, however, in the poetry of Francisco Brines where this complicity is directly interrogated. This questioning is especially evident in the opening poem of Brines's 1977 collection, *Insistencias en Luzbel*. In "Esplendor negro" (Black splendor) (*ED* 203– 4) an answer is sought to the underlying query of the poem, the collection, and all of Brines's poetry: What is knowledge? In "Esplendor negro," this epistemological quest is itself a question because the search for the grounds of knowledge is also a critique of both knowing and expressing what is known.[15] It is this quest(ioning) that underlies not only "Esplendor negro" but also Brines's poetry of the last three decades and, importantly, the poetry of the group to which he belongs. Brines's poetry, as we shall see, is paradigmatic of the process of poetry demonstrating "un conocimiento haciéndose" (knowledge becoming) its own *différance*. Viewed as such, Brines's "Esplendor negro" synecdochically represents the quest for knowledge manifested in many works of the members of this group, a quest that also involves the questioning not only of the nature of knowledge itself but also of the language used to describe this quest:

> Sólo una vez pudiste conocer aquel Esplendor negro,
> e intermitentemente recuerdas la experiencia con vaguedad,
> aproximaciones difusas, inminencias,
> y así, desde tu juventud, arrastras frío,
> un invisible manto de ceniza escarlata.   5
> Y no fue necesario cegar los ojos,
> pues de las luces claras de los astros
> llegó el delirio aquel, la posibilidad más exacta y sencilla:
> en vez de Dios o el mundo
> aquel negro Esplendor,   10
> que ni siquiera es punto, pues no hay en él espacio,
> ni se puede nombrar, porque no se dilata.
> Valen igual Serenidad y Vértigo,
> pues las palabras están dichas desde la noche de la tierra,
> y las palabras son tan sólo expresión de un engaño.   15
> Volver al centro aquel es ir por las afueras de la vida,
> sin conocer la vida, un no mundo imposible,
> pues sólo el no nacer te pudiera acercar a esa experiencia.

Crear la inexistencia y su totalidad,
no te hizo poderoso,   20
ni derramó tu llanto, y nada redimiste.
La misma incomprensión que contemplar el mundo
te produjo el terror de aquel Esplendor negro,
y aquel desvalimiento al cubrirte las sábanas.

Only once did you manage to know that black Splendor,
and intermittently you recall the experience with vagueness,
diffuse approximations, imminences,
and so, since your youth, you drag along,
an invisible, cold cloak of scarlet ash.   5
And it was not necessary to blind your eyes,
inasmuch as from the clear light of the stars
arrived that delirium, the most exact and the simplest possibility:
instead of God or the world
that black Splendor,   10
that is not even a point, since in it there is no space,
nor can it be named, because it does not expand.
Serenity and Vertigo are worth the same,
since words are said from the night of the land,
and words are only the expression of deceit.   15
To return to that center is to go along the outskirts of life,
without knowing life, an impossible nonworld,
since only not being born could bring you close to that experience.
Creating nonexistence and its totality,
did not make you powerful,   20
nor did it scatter your weeping, and you redeemed nothing.
The very incomprehension that contemplating the world
produced in you dread of that black Splendor,
and that helplessness upon covering yourself with sheets.

The progress of the poem depends on the unfolding of a series of answers to the fundamental query. At first, the text introduces its *tú*-protagonist (you), perhaps a poet-writer, as an example of someone who, at least on one occasion, managed to acquire knowledge, even though this knowledge was obtained with the assistance of the darkened understanding or, viewed another way, the obscured poetic inspiration of "aquel Esplendor negro" (that black Splendor) (line 1).[16] Recollection of the process of coming to know (line 2) and the past as a vehicle for knowing (lines 4–5) follow as possible answers.

The answering pattern changes in lines 6–12 when the text provides a series of examples of knowledge taken from the tradition of Western philosophical thought. Knowledge is "Dios" (God) (line 9), divine wisdom, divine illumination, the center or source of all knowledge. Knowledge is "el mundo" (the world) (line 9), where knowledge is viewed as esthesis. These two possible answers are then substituted by a third: "aquel negro Esplendor" (that black Splendor) (line 10), a variation of the object that came to be known by the *tú* in the opening line. There is no overall simple, exact response to the poem's underlying question, even though line 8 asserts the opposite. There is only, and always, insufficient understanding, characterized in the poem in terms of metaphoric light and darkness.[17]

Another possible answer presented by the text is that of propositional knowledge, or knowledge expressed by words (lines 14–15). At first, the *logos*[18] is viewed as a mediating element enabling the end result of coming to know "aquel Esplendor negro" (lines 1, 6–10). In lines 14–15, however, this example is refuted by the subsequent claim that what is known cannot be encompassed in a single expression or summarily described. Propositional knowledge, thus, is dismissed as a possible answer to the poem's underlying query.[19]

The protagonist's developing skepticism is more and more pronounced as the closing examples unfold. Both as one who seeks knowledge and as a writer who attempts to express what is known with words, the *tú* is filled with wisdom that is forever obfuscated. The protagonist's illumination does not lead to understanding, rather it leads to "dread" of repeatedly experiencing doubt: "La misma incomprensión que contemplar el mundo, / te produjo el terror de aquel Esplendor negro, / y aquel desvalimiento al cubrirte las sábanas" (The very incomprehension that contemplating the world / produced in you dread of that black Splendor, / and that helplessness upon covering yourself with sheets) (lines 22–23). Doubting both the possibility for and the expression of knowledge, the protagonist presents a twofold, interwoven answer to the underlying question of the poem: knowledge is impossible and "las palabras son tan sólo expresión de un engaño" (words are only the expression of deceit) (line 15).[20]

The interpretation of "Esplendor negro" advanced above is based on the opening assertion of the poem: "Sólo una vez pudiste conocer aquel Esplendor negro." Its starting point originates in the positive declaration that the *tú*-protagonist not only tried but also successfully managed to come to know "aquel Esplendor negro." If we view this figure as personification, the preterite tense of the auxiliary verb *poder* further stresses that the *tú* succeeded in meeting and becoming acquainted with "aquel Esplendor negro."

A discrepancy arises, however, when the critic questions the verbal phrase "pudiste conocer." The etymological root of the verb *conocer*, the Latin *cognoscere*, conveys the process of coming to know, of investigating, of learning by inquiring (*H* 362). This cognitive *process*, however, both abruptly comes to an end and all at once begins since "conocer," functioning as the verbal complement of the auxiliary verb "pudiste," assumes a preterite or perfected meaning. A further complication arises when the critic notes that the presence of "conocer" in the text is marked by absence because when it appears in the poem's first line, "conocer" is not marked grammatically for subject, time, and manner of action, and thus it depends on the auxiliary verb, "pudiste," to supplement these. In addition, as a transitive verb it requires its own object complement. Conceptually and figuratively speaking, *conocer* lacks the understanding, the direct awareness and the ability to discern that is denotatively associated with this verb since what comes to be known is the equivocal, uncertain, questionable "Esplendor negro."

Even though the "process" of coming to know has been limited by the presence of the preterite of the verb *poder*, it could be argued that, after all, knowledge has been attained, as the opening line declares. But what was/is known? A possible answer lies in the opening assertion: "Sólo una vez pudiste conocer aquel Esplendor negro." When the critic interprets the figure "Esplendor negro" as the doubt engendered by the protagonist's skepticism, a view sustained by the first reading of the poem, a question arises. What ultimately was known, upon either completing or beginning the process of knowing, if what was known, ultimately, is Doubt?

The opening assertion leads to further complications. Scrutinizing the verb *pudiste*, the critic finds that at its very root the verb implies "to have power" (*H* 1404).[21] Although the poem's protagonist seems to be endowed with the power and the ability to know, what is known remains inexact (line 1). The critic can, however, look at the underlying potential of the verb *poder* in yet another way. As a verb of incomplete predication, *poder* requires a complement. In one sense, then, *conocer* gives to *poder* something it did not originally have: understanding of the ability to know, even though what is known is uncertain. Thus, the semantic sense of *poder* leads the critic to believe that mastery of "conocer" not only is possible but also, as the preterite verb "pudiste" implies, has occurred. This mastery, however, is incomplete because it depends on an act of knowing that, in itself, forever is shadowed by "aquel Esplendor negro." As the supplemental accomplice of knowledge, ignorance makes understanding (im)possible.

For the *tú* of the poem, any advance in wisdom is simultaneously a movement of the mind inward and outward: "Volver al centro aquel es ir por las afueras de la vida" (To return to that center is to go along the outskirts of life) (line 16). To progress in coming to know is to regress: "sin conocer la vida, un no mundo imposible" (without knowing life, an impossible nonworld) (line 17). The mind, opened and infused with the dim flash of "aquel Esplendor negro," becomes aware of the obscured illumination of incommutable truth-error. Both marking the conflictual structure of opposition *and* the interval between inversion, the figure "aquel Esplendor negro" manifests the "irruptive emergence of a new 'concept'" (*POS* 42): the moment of suspended illumination *and* suspended ignorance.

Possession of such "knowledge" leads the text's protagonist to "dread," (line 23) perhaps because the *tú*, despite the declaration "pudiste conocer," teeters on the edge of illumination *and* ignorance. The text's protagonist discovers that the search leads to direct cognition of what is known *and* what is not known. The claim of managing to know, "pudiste conocer," the starting point of the poem's argument, is problematized by the presence of "aquel Esplendor negro." Knowledge of what is known leads not to answering the text's fundamental question but rather to questioning the epistemological ground of the text.

From the apparently inappropriate substitution of one word for another arises an additional concept appropriately marked by *différance*. Perhaps abusing the real functioning of substitution with the misuse of words, the catachrestic "aquel Esplendor negro" emphasizes the work of supplementarity adding to *and* replacing the concept of knowledge.[22] No longer viewed as the condition for understanding or as the condition for apprehending truth, "pudiste conocer" remains suspended between illumination and ignorance, light and darkness, truth and error.

In "Esplendor negro," and in other poems of *Insistencias en Luzbel*, the quest for wisdom is also a questioning of the grounds from which the quest begins. In this search, language is not the means by which understanding is mastered, but rather the means by which the impossibility of complete understanding is explored: "pues las palabras están dichas desde la noche de la tierra, / y las palabras son tan sólo expresión de un engaño" (since words are said from the night of the land, / and words are only the expression of deceit) (lines 14 –15). This moment of suspension within the text, where the poem comments on its own medium, marks what J. Hillis Miller aptly terms "the linguistic moment" and as such "breaks the illusion that language is a transparent medium of meaning" (*Linguistic Moment* xiv). Foregrounding undecidable conceptual elements in the text, such as the titular catachresis, "Esplendor negro," and the repetition of this metonymy, sometimes in variation (line 10), emphasizes the poem's central problem: "referentiality in language is a fiction" (J. Hillis Miller, "Stevens' Rock" II, 29). Or, to use the words of the poet in "Definición de la nada" (Definition of nothingness) (*IEL, ED* 205), "hablamos desde la ficción de la palabra" (we speak from the fiction of the word) (line 6). Viewed as such,

"Esplendor negro" is a critique, a testing of the concept, scope and validity of both knowledge *and* meaning.

The opening claim, "Sólo una vez pudiste conocer aquel Esplendor negro," is refuted in another linguistic moment of the text when the *tú*, it seems, encounters difficulty in writing, in naming, in coming to know through naming: "ni se puede nombrar, porque no se dilata" (nor can it be named, because it does not expand)(line 12). Despite his profession as a writer and the opening assertion of the poem, the *tú* realizes that naming is not within his grasp, perhaps because poetic inspiration is obscured due to the specter of "aquel Esplendor negro," or perhaps also because "las palabras son tan sólo expresión de un engaño" (line 15). Throughout "Esplendor negro," the act of naming undermines the power to know by naming.

Despite the claim made in line 12, "no se puede nombrar," "aquel Esplendor negro" has been named (line 1). Catachresis, however, problematizes not only the assumption underlying "no se puede nombrar" but also that of the poem's initial assertion. The text goes on to show that in this naming, "aquel Esplendor negro" is substituted for other designations such as "Dios o el mundo" (God or the world) (line 9). The denomination is further qualified by the adjective "negro" and thus made to be different from other possible manifestations of brightness, brilliance and luster, as the Latin root *splendor* implies. The "power" to name, recalling the etymological sense of the verb *poder*, is undermined, however, both by the presence of "no" ("no se puede nombrar") and by the work of the supplement that undoes the binary opposition *Esplendor/negro*.[23] "No se puede nombrar" is further undermined by textuality, for in the semantic weave of the the Spanish verb *nombrar*, and the underlying Latin *nominari*, is enmeshed the root *gno* (whence *gnosco, nosco* [H 1213, 1216]), and, thus, the etymological thread "to begin to know." Once again the trace ensures the constant vacillation of meanings as it subverts the possibility of mastery of knowledge through language.

In "Esplendor negro," the poetic text is conceived as a critical inquiry where answers are indeterminate and questions become conundrums. In retracing this text, the critic repeats, questions, clarifies and obfuscates even further the critical inquiry begun by the poet in the poetic text.[24] Driven by "aquel Esplendor negro," the critic investigates not only its role in the poetic text but also its dissemination in the interpretive text.[25] Suspended between illumination and darkness, knowledge and ignorance, answers and queries, the critical text repeatedly seeks its own ground while simultaneously engaged in the act of critiquing that ground. As it turns out, this search for ground often finds itself both without ground and on "groundless ground," to borrow J. Hillis Miller's words (*Linguistic Moment* 433), for the critic, like the poet, lacks the power to master knowledge ("pudiste conocer" line 1) through language ("las palabras son tan sólo expresión de un engaño" line 15). Writing, both the poet and the critic discover, is not a way of knowing but rather a means by which the questioning of knowing, meaning, and the meaning of knowing takes place. The critic's inquiry, like that of the poet's, charts the ceaseless movement of *différance* which, as Johnson urges, "is not a 'concept' or 'idea' that is 'truer' than presence. It can only be a process of textual *work*, a strategy of *writing*" (Introduction xvi).

Since deconstruction, as Anderson points out, "investigates the nature and production of knowledge" (137), it can be viewed as a method particularly well adapted to this critic's inquiry into poetry and criticism concerned with knowledge. Knowledge is not *the* issue of deconstruction, nor of deconstructive reading. Rather, deconstruction questions the scope, the concept, the production of knowledge as the basis of mastery, power, authority. Viewed as such, deconstruction "examines the force of power and authority in the text as a desire for mastery—the attempt to master knowledge through language, and meaning through interpretation—a desire that textuality ultimately subverts, for writing always already has begun to deconstruct itself" (Anderson 138).

In this search for and critique of epistemological ground, the critic, in considering deconstructively the interrelation between text and interpretation, discovers that in interrogating Rodríguez's "Alto jornal," Valente's "Primer poema," and Brines's "Esplendor negro," dissemination is born in language and writing, like the medium it uses, is duplicitous. As a critical attitude, as a way of cross-examining knowledge and meaning, the deconstructive readings presented here call into question the ground of knowledge, the process of cognitive discovery, and the ground of language. Poetry, like criticism, is not a process of knowing but rather a method for questioning the activity of coming to know. Repeatedly, the poet and the critic are forced to explore in writing a series of queries concerned with the nature of knowledge and the nature of language, queries that more often than not lead to an impasse. Both the poetic text and the critical text, thus, forever point to epistemological and linguistic problems obstinately refusing singular, unequivocal solutions. For Francisco Brines, and for many of the other poets frequently associated with his group, suspended ignorance foregrounds knowledge in such a way that what is known remains (in)exact. Deconstruction, like the poetic texts it questions, calls attention to knowing that is not knowing and writing that both keeps textuality forever in play and always already points to its own deconstructability.

2
(Un)Tangling "The Weave of Time"

> . . . Sólo el vacío
> fue el tejido del tiempo en este llano . . .
>
> . . . Only the void was the weave of time on this plane . . .
> —Francisco Brines

> The critic cannot unscramble the tangle of lines of meaning,
> comb its threads out so they shine clearly side by side. He
> can only retrace the text, set its elements in motion once
> more, in that experience of the failure of determinable
> reading which is so decisive here.　　　—J. Hillis Miller

One could assert that much of Francisco Brines's poetry is an account of time. More precisely, it is an account of human being's consciousness of time within or from the perspective of human existence.[1] Just as Brines's poetry asks "What is knowledge?" in a similiar fashion his poems and their speakers often ask "What is time?" This latter, underlying question, although asked in a seemingly straightforward manner, is never answered directly in Brines's poetry. The reader might expect and even pursue a single, conclusive response to the query "What is time?" however, no such determinate response is encountered. On the contrary, it is the knotted concept of time together with human being's consciousness of time, and not a simplistic definition of the concept, that Brines's poetry has probed incessantly since 1960.

The complexity of the temporal issue central to Brines's poetry is itself reflected in the multifaceted descriptions of and approaches to this issue offered by the poet in his poetry and in his various *poéticas* of the last three decades. The critic, in approaching Brines's numerous approaches to human consciousness of time, might attempt to sort these descriptions out from the many and varying texts into which they have been interwoven. Here, the hope would be that if such accounts and appraisals of time were separated out from the temporal tangle of Brines's numerous texts then, perhaps, the perplexing problem of time would be greatly simplified, more clearly defined, and, ultimately, better understood.

Another strategy the critic might adopt could involve searching for the "center" of the "tejido del tiempo" (the weave of time) ("El triunfo del amor" [The triumph of love], lines 6–7, *ED* 157) that is Brines's poetry. Even the most cursory first reading of Brines's poetic collections reveals this poet's keenly acute awareness of a specific temporal moment, the present instant. While engaged in this quest, the critic quickly comes to realize that the present moment figures prominently among the interlaced temporal threads of the complexly intricate, textual "weave" of Brines's poetry. Within this brief temporal interval the poet spins the story of human living while writing the poetic text. The numerous poetic voices heard throughout Brines's various collections construct and reconstruct the poet's consciousness of the present instant as each, speaking within and about this fleeting moment, experiences and recounts the ephemeral nature of human existence and writing about human existence. The critic's own act of examining this interwoven center of the textual mesh occurs *within* the very temporal instant under scrutiny, thus highlighting it even more each time the quest(ioning) of the multiple, interlaced threads of the Brinesean "weave of time" takes place.

This critic will engage in both critical strategies here in an attempt to trace and retrace the threads enmeshed in this textual-temporal-existential "weave of time." The critic, first, will attempt to card, to disentangle, to collect together the numerous thematic fibers constituting the woven, temporal texts of Brines's poetry in order to spin her/his own interpretive web. The first critical strategy, then, will involve sorting out various thematic, temporal strands in an attempt at finding a single thread that will point to an answer to one of the fundamental questions underlying Brines's poetry: "What is time?" We shall see, however, that in the interpretive act the critic's attempt to disentangle this complexly intricate, textual-temporal weave only tangles each separated, thematic thread again and again in the entanglement of temporal themes that is Brines's poetry.

The second strategy will involve questioning the center of Brines's textual, temporal weave: the present instant. Here, interrogation of the question "What is time?" leads to other questions in the supplementary series of questions concerning time often raised by various poetic voices in Brines's poetry: "What is the present?" "What is the present instant?" "What is the conscious present?" This interrogation, as we shall see, leads the critic to "el fragilísimo presente" (the very fragile present) (*SP* 41), that specious, temporal moment wavering end-lessly with the past.

As the critical act of unweaving begins, an observation offered in the poet's "La certidumbre de la poesía" (The certainty of poetry), which serves as the introduction to *Selección propia*, captures what could be considered, perhaps, to be Brines's most revealing yet at the same time concealing answer to the question "What is time?": "El hombre sigue siendo la misma débil trama del tiempo y ante él se presenta el mismo vacío o esperanza" (Man [humankind] continues being that same weak woof of time and before him that same void or hope presents itself) (*SP* 41).[2] By viewing human being as a "woof of time," Brines's poetic texts, as the etymological source *textus* discloses, are themselves weaves (*OED* 3274) into which are interlaced multiple, differentiating accounts of the temporal skein of human existence. In this same prose commentary, Brines offers another view of time: "El tiempo es mi cuer-po y mi enigma, y también el fracaso definitivo" (Time is my body and my enigma, and also the determinate destruction) (*SP* 20). For this poet, time constitutes and reconstitutes human existence whenever human being engages in living. But what is living? For the speaker of "El visitante me abrazó, de nuevo" (The visitor embraced me, again), one of Brines's early poems from *Las brasas* (*ED* 22–23), living is marked by human being's futile attempts to recollect and relive "la juventud ya lejos" (now distant youth) (line 12). The transitory nature of youth and the useless act of attempting to revive and recapture it are also examined in "Días de invierno en la casa de verano" (Winter days in the summer house), from Brines's most recent *El otoño de las rosas* (lines 10–15, *OR* 15–17):

> Vivo en la intimidad de la casa vacía,
> y en las habitaciones despobladas
> puedo escuchar el sonido apagado de la vida,
> tocar un tiempo helado,
> gustar en los espejos un insulso sabor,
> el tedio de una imagen sin juventud.

> I dwell in the intimacy of the empty house,
> and in the uninhabited rooms
> I can hear the extinguished sound of life,
> touch a frigid time,
> taste in the mirrors a tasteless taste,
> the tediousness of an image without youth.

In this poem, however, in contrast to "El visitante me abrazó, de nuevo," the poem's speaker comes to learn that it is better to have lived, despite

the transitory nature of human existence in time, than never to have
lived at all, as the closing lines reveal:

> Con todo, en este invierno tan lejano,
> hay un calor de vida ya gastada,
> la seca aceptación del mal o la alegría,
> un secreto entusiasmo de haber sido.

> Nevertheless, in this so distant winter,
> there is a warmth from life now consumed,
> the acceptance of harm or happiness,
> a secret enthusiasm for having been.   (lines 56–59)

As the critic attempts to trace the threads in the Brinesean "weave
of time" she/he encounters other thematic strands that could also serve
as answers to the question "What is time?" The speakers and characters populating Brines's poetry frequently think of time as an element
that flows or as a medium through which human beings and human
actions advance. Time is thus viewed as passage, as movement, as transition, from one segment in the day to the next, from one day to the next,
from one year to the next, from one season of the year to the next, from
one stage in human being's life to the next, from present to future, from
life to death, etc.. Time as passage is one of the most prevalent temporal motifs in Brines's poetry. The speaker of "Los ocios ganados"
(Acquired pastimes) (10), from *El otoño de las rosas*, observes, for
example, that time is mysteriously slipping away: "Y en este día de
septiembre lento / todo es ganado, salvo que he perdido / un día de mi
vida para siempre" (And on this slow September day / all is won, except
that I have lost / a day of my life forever) (lines 10 –12). Some twenty
years earlier in *Palabras a la oscuridad*, the speaker of "Oscureciendo
el bosque" (The darkening forest) (ED 95–96) contemplates the
ephemeral nature of reality within the flow of time. In this poem the
advent of twilight in a forest leads the first-person speaker to question
the larger, all-encompassing, metaphoric encroachment of death on
life, as the poem's opening moment reveals:

> Toda esta hermosa tarde, de poca luz
> caída sobre los grises bosques de Inglaterra,
> es tiempo.
>   Tiempo que está muriendo
> dentro de mis tranquilos ojos,   5
> mezclándose en el tiempo que se extingue.
> Es en la vida todo

transcurrir natural hacia la muerte,
y el gratuito don que es ser, y respirar,
respira y es hacia la nada angosta.   10

All of this lovely afternoon, of very little light
fallen on England's grey forests,
is time.
              Time that is dying
within my tranquil eyes,   5
blending with the time that is being extinguished.
In life all
naturally runs its course toward death,
and the gratuitous gift that is life, and breathing,
breathes and exists toward the narrow nothingness.   10

In Brines's poetry, the theme of time as passage often becomes inter-twined with the idea that events, be they future or present, are forever receding into the past. Time is thus viewed as change, where all ele-ments of reality are in constant, ceaseless flux. The Heraclitean notion of change and of the unity of opposites resulting from change underlie Brines's vision of reality in *Aún no*, in particular.[3] For the poet, reali-ty and the language used to mirror it are represented as a dynamic unity of opposites where, within each momentary phase of the perceiving of reality, of the capturing of the perception in poetic form, and of the reading of the poem itself, opposite is transformed into opposite and the nature and the unity of reality and the poem come to be known. This process is especially evident in "Noche" (Night) (*ED* 190), "Extinción" (Extinction) (*ED* 160), "Sombrío ardor" (Somber ardor) (*ED* 161), "La ronda del aire" (The hovering air) (*ED* 183–84), and "Todavía el tiem-po" (Nevertheless time) (*ED* 186), to name but a few.[4]

Change as a pervasive feature of temporal reality is a constant the-matic feature of many Brinesean collections. The notion that only change is real is evident in the poem "Oscureciendo el bosque," espe-cially in the lines cited earlier, and also in the poem "Otoño inglés" (English autumn) (*ED* 105–6), also from *Palabras a la oscuridad:* "Es ley fatal del mundo / que toda vida acabe en podredumbre" (The fatal law of the world is / that all life ends in decay) (lines 35–36). Fre-quently in this 1966 collection, the dual and complementary notions of time as change and life as a continuous passing are linked, as is evident in "Amor en Agrigento" (Love in Agrigento) (*ED* 116 –17), when past love, a city and her temples of antiquity, and twilight all converge to reveal: "éste es el tránsito de la muerte, confundiéndose con la vida" (this is the transit of death, being mistaken for life) (line 24). The tem-poral stuff of personal, human existence, as the poetry of *Insistencias en Luzbel* often discloses, is summarized in this way in the poem "Epitafio del vivo" (Epitaph of the living) (*ED* 223): "Soy misterioso: sufro, y no me quedo" (I am mysterious: I suffer, and I do not remain) (line 1). Or, as the speaker of "Resumen fantástico" (Fantastic summary) (*ED* 227), well-grounded in his everydayness, succinctly puts it: "Hemos quemado muchos cigarillos, / y así se fue la vida" (We have smoked many cigarettes, / and that is how life slipped away) (lines 1–2).

The critic as card can also disentangle and then collect together other thematic strands in this textual, temporal weave under scrutiny. Throughout Brines's poetry, and also in his various *poéticas*, the poet often tries to combat time as passage and time as change by writing, what he has termed, "poesía de salvación" (poetry of salvation) (*SP* 18). According to Brines, this type of poetry "intenta revivir la pasión de la vida, traer de nuevo a la experiencia lo que, por estar vivo, ha condenado el tiempo, de hacer que el instante transcurra sin pasar, efímero y eterno a la vez. Y con el instante, el suceder del hombre. No importa que se trate de una ilusión" (intends to relive the passion of life, to re-experience that which, by being alive, time has condemned, to make the instant pass without passing, at once ephemeral and eternal. And with the instant, the happening of humankind. It is not important that it may concern an illusion) (*SP* 18). A little later in this discussion Brines elaborates further on "poetry of salvation," explaining:

> Una de las motivaciones más frecuentes en mí . . . es la necesidad de ese intento desvalido de fijar el tiempo que se nos escapa, de salvar esos momentos de dicha o de dolor que tan precariamente nos pertenecen y que, en definitiva, somos nosotros mismos. Creo que el conjunto de mi obra, aun en los momentos en que aparece el cántico, no es otra cosa que una extensa elegía. (*SP* 24)

> One of my most frequent themes . . . is the necessity of that helpless attempt at trying to fix the time that escapes us, to save those moments of happiness or pain that so precariously pertain to us and that, in conclusion, are ourselves. I believe that the whole of my work, even in the moments in which the canticle appears, is nothing other than an extensive elegy.

The act of unraveling Brines's poetry and *poéticas* often takes the critic to irreconcilably different thematic threads in the temporal weave. On the one hand, the critic encounters thematic strands where the poet and his speakers attempt "to fix the time that escapes" human being in the course of living. Yet, at the same time, the critic also finds numerous thematic threads exhibiting time as ceaseless duration, unmeasurable, eternal. In Brines's poetry, time conceived and experienced as duration often takes two specific forms: memory and writing. Each method aids the poet in his various attempts at and repeated struggles with coming to terms with transient existence. For many of Brines's poetic voices, "La memoria es de vidrio; nos ayuda: / congela, enturbia el tiempo" (Memory is made of glass; it helps us: / time congeals, muddies") (lines 31–32, "Reminiscencias" [Reminiscences], *AN, ED* 189). For others, "la memoria turba / un reino frío y solitario y vasto" (memory disturbs / a cold kingdom solitary and vast) (lines 29–30, "El mendigo" [The beggar], *PO, ED* 143).

The act of remembering past events, especially those events associated with youth and love, is one method employed by the poet as he attempts not only to recover the past through his speakers within his poetry but also to bring the past forward in time so that it might continue into the present by means of the act of writing.[5] At times, this recovery of the past brings with it great happiness, as "Tiempo y espacio del amor" (Time and space of love), from *El otoño de las rosas* (33) reveals:

> . . . Lejanos,
> nos poblará el recuerdo del amor,
> me llegará en el sueño tu mágica visita,
> y aún te amaré más. (lines 10–13)

> . . . Distant,
> the memory of love will fill us,
> in dreams your magical visit will come to me,
> and I shall love you even more.

At other times, however, recollection of the past involves intense pain, especially when the poem's speaker learns "queda sólo un recuerdo que se muere / con más prisa esta vez / que otros recuerdos rotos . . ." (only a dying memory remains / this time more hurriedly / than other broken memories. . .) (lines 26–28, "El huésped," [The guest], *OR* 24).

In many of Brines's poems the act of writing poetry becomes synonymous with time viewed as continuance. In "Días finales" (Final days) of *Insistencias en Luzbel* (*ED* 240), for example, writing captures the memory of "Todo muere / sobre este mundo vivo" (All dies / in this living world) (lines 2–3). This method, however, as the poem's speaker later admits "es el último engaño de su vida" (is the ultimate deceit of his life) (line 29). "Poetry of salvation," poetry used to combat time as passage, is highlighted in "Salvación en la oscuridad" (Salvation in the darkness) (*ED* 221), from *Insistencias en Luzbel*. Here, writing itself is viewed as an act of salvaging happiness that could be lost forever in time. In the poem "Al lector" (To the reader) (*ED* 215), also from Brines's 1977 collection, the speaker-writer comes to learn about an important aspect of both his own existence and of the work he is creating. While engaged in the act of writing poetry, this speaker comprehends that writing is itself an appeal to the reader to continue the existence of both the poem and the poet. Writing and reading, thus, are viewed as interdependent acts of continuance that, to use Brines's words, underscore the "necesidad de afirmar la vida en contra de lo que la niega" (the necessity of affirming life against all that negates it) (*SP* 48).[6]

Another aspect of time as duration explored by some of the speakers of Brines's poetry is that of cyclical time where vital elements of nature perpetually renew themselves each spring. The eternal return of life within nature is the central motif of "Isla de piedras" (Island of stones), from *Palabras a la oscuridad* (*ED* 97–98). Here, for example, human being's own temporality is contraposed to the continuance of natural life. Often, but not always, in *El otoño de las rosas,* flowers are associated with cyclical time and the eternal return of new life within nature. Many of the poems of this collection are filled with the speaker's lingering experience of the persistent fragrance of jasmine, honeysuckle, orange blossoms, wild roses, bougainvillea, and roses. Time as continuance and the repetition of life within this continuance is a fundamental theme of Brines's latest collection. The speaker of "Un olor de azahar" (A fragrance of citrus blossoms) (20–22), for example, comes to comprehend that even though in his own lifetime "busco la mentida eternidad / aún (hoy sé que todo es tiempo negro)" (I search for deceptive eternity / still [today I know that all is black time]) (lines 9–10), in nature no such deception exists since, as the poem's final moment reveals, "Y acaso, si hay fortuna, algo recobre: / este cálido olor bajo la luna, / la primavera del naranjo blanco" (And maybe, if there is good fortune, something may be recovered: / this warm fragrance under the moon, / the springtime of the white orange-tree) (lines 42–44).

There are still other thematic threads the critic could attempt to sort out from the Brinesean textual, temporal weave. For example, Brines has written: "El tiempo es mi cuerpo y mi enigma, y también el fracaso definitivo; el amor es mi inserción en el tiempo con la intensidad máxima, el deseo de mi mejor realización posible, y es también un fracaso que, aunque no tan absoluto como el de la mortalidad, puede ser más doloroso" (Time is my body and my enigma, and also the determinate destruction; love is my insertion into time with maximum intensity, the desire of my best possible realization, and it is also a destruction that, although not as absolute as that of mortality, can be more painful) (*SP* 20). Many of the speakers of Brines's poems, while experiencing and attempting to comprehend the transitory nature of human existence, often turn to the revitalizing act of loving where love, according to the speaker of "Días de invierno en la casa de verano" (Winter days in the summer house) (*OR* 16), is viewed as "el mejor remedio a quien estaba / perdiendo ya la vida" (the best remedy for someone / who is now losing life) (lines 40 – 41). Love as the poetic speakers' "insertion into time" takes many forms in Brines's poetry. In "Ladridos jadeantes en el césped" (Panting howls on the lawn), from *Las brasas* (*ED* 24 –25), for example, love is intimately linked to eternal time and cyclical renovation within human existence. "Canción de los cuerpos" (Song of the bodies), from *Insistencias en Luzbel* (*ED* 231), "Envío del recién llegado" (Dispatch of the recently arrived) (34), "El triunfo de la carne" (The triumph of the flesh) (80 – 81), and "Los veranos" (The summers) (91), from *El otoño de las rosas*, reveal that in love, and especially in the carnal act, the poem's speaker is able to experience and reexperience youth, both the youth of the lover and the past youth of the speaker. The poetic voice heard in "El triunfo de la carne," however, like other Brinesean characters in the story of love that unfolds in many of his poems, comes to learn that his "insertion into time" by means of the carnal act proves futile.[7]

In "Encuentro urbano" (Urban encounter), from *Poemas excluidos* (Excluded poems) (*PE* 16 –17), the poet, in engaging in the activity of writing, seeks to recover, recollect, resuscitate an amorous experience that has since been lost to the past in the course of living.[8] Recollection of past love through and by means of writing is not only a frequent motif in Brines's love poetry but also a way for the poetic speakers to continue to reexperience the temporal, amorous experience, thereby witnessing and coming to know time as continuance. The speaker of "La realidad no permanece" (Reality does not last) (*ED* 233), from *Insistencias en Luzbel*, however, learns that memory, like love, is only temporal:

> Esta revuelta tarde me lleva a Bath
> y a ti, pero no a la ciudad de reposadas
> calles, ni a quien tú debes ser en el día de hoy.
> La habitación se agranda en la penumbra
> mientras llueve en la calle suavemente.   5
> Hay en la chimenea, un fuego que calienta
> nuestros cuerpos desnudos, y que alumbra
> el vasto espacio con insuficiencia.
> . . . .
> una tarde tan larga en Bath,   22
> que penetró en la noche, hasta las luces rotas
> de un día casi eterno.

Aquella habitación que, acaso, guarda ahora
sólo el recuerdo vivo de un único habitante:
ese que contemplaba, desde un lecho vacío   27
la escasa realidad de un destruido fuego.

This unsettling afternoon takes me to Bath
and to you, but not to the city of quiet
streets, nor to whom you must be today.
The room becomes bigger in the penumbra
while it softly rains in the street.   5
There is, in the chimney, a fire that warms
our nude bodies, illuminating
the vast space with insufficiency.

.   .   .   .

a long afternoon in Bath,   22
that penetrated the night, as far as the broken lights
of an almost eternal day.
The room that, hardly, now keeps
only the living memories of its single inhabitant:
that one who used to contemplate, from the empty bed,   27
the scanty reality of a destroyed passion.

What has the critic learned from this attempted unweaving of "el tejido del tiempo" that is Brines's poetry? Despite this disentangling, this
sorting, one still cannot come up with a singular, thematic thread defining the concept of time not only because, as we have just witnessed,
none is self-evident within the differing and deferring poetic texts but
also because the many temporal views presented are, in fact, often contradictory, decidedly heterogeneous, and irreconcilably different. We
have just seen, for example, that some of Brines's speakers contend that
time is lasting continuance while others focus on time as passage.
Some both witness and find consolation in the perpetuity of nature
while yet other dissonant voices lament the transience of natural elements in time. For others, human being's incessant desire for immortality only serves to highlight, often painfully, "nuestro destino mortal" (our mortal destiny) (*SP* 20). Some speakers view memory as a
means to combat human temporality; yet memory is not a fail-safe
method for recovering what has been lost because, as the poetic voice
of "Un olor de azahar" (A fragrance of citrus blossoms) (*OR* 22) recalls,
"Cuando llegue el olvido, la memoria / rastreará esta dicha para nada"
(When oblivion arrives, memory / will trace this happiness for naught)
(lines 40 – 41). Love is often presented as a "remedio" (remedy) ("Días
de invierno en la casa de verano" [Winter days in the summer house],
line 40, *OR* 16) for human temporality, a way for human beings to

"insert" (*SP* 20) themselves into time and momentarily "fijar el tiempo que se nos escapa" (fix the time that escapes us) (*SP* 24). However, other voices in Brines's poetry view love as a transitory act or event. Still others see love continually affirming the cyclical nature of time. Some speakers view the act of writing as a form of continuance, while others see this same act as a transient effort utilizing "las palabras borradas que fueron nuestra vida" (erased words that were our life) ("Las noches de abandono" [Nights of abandonment], *AN*, *ED* 193).

Both Brines's prose and poetic texts, thus, continually constitute and reconstitute differing and deferring versions of the concept of time, differing and deferring accounts of the medium of time, that "general medium in which all events take place in succession or appear to take place in succession" (*Dictionary of Philosophy* 318). In this poetry, as the attempted unweaving of the Brinesean "tejido del tiempo" demonstrates, the critic does not encounter a determinate answer to the fundamental query entwined in this temporal skein. Instead, this unraveling of the textual mesh itself points to the raveled questioning undertaken by poet and critic alike as each attempts to disentangle the numerous thematic threads of "el tejido del tiempo."

How, then, should we enter the labyrinthine weave of Brines's texts? Whenever attempts are made to thread through the entire temporal tangle, as this critic has just done, the concept of time is not simplified, as one might have hoped, but rather, it becomes more and more complicated. As we just saw, untangling the temporal skein only tangled it up again because the critic did not arrive at a single, explicit definition of time, even though Brines's speakers often tried to convince her/him that such a definition might be both possible and eventually forthcoming in the poetic text. Another approach might be to sort out various intertextual strands tinted with matters of interest to traditional Western metaphysics. In this way, many of Brines's observations on time as passage, time as change, and time as duration, for example, could be intertwined with Western philosophical thought. The critic could trace some of the ideas and notions of time presented in Brines's poetry to texts of St. Augustine, Heraclitus, Friedrich Nietszche, and Henri Bergson, to mention but a few. Such an intertextual unweaving, however, only would provide, at best, textual affiliations.

Perhaps another strategy, that of examining closely *a single*, thematic, temporal thread, might be employed. By isolating only one theme, for example time as passage, from the mesh into which it is entwined, one could hope that the entire knotted problem of time might be better understood. In Brines's poetry, however, no singular, temporal theme really can be successfully isolated because, as we have seen in this critic's aborted attempt at untangling, it stubbornly remains enmeshed in the temporal-textual tangle. Time as passage perpetually interimplicates time as continuance, just as temporal change and transcience forever shadow temporal perpetuity.[9]

How, then, could the critic enter the "tejido del tiempo" of Brines's poetry? One other way that will be attempted here is not to enter the weave in quest of sorting out from the entire mesh a single, thematic strand but rather to enter by questioning the thematic threads themselves. This could involve following not one thematic thread to the center of the Brinesean "weave of time," but rather scrutinizing closely those interlaced threads constituting the center of the textual tapestry. The critic, thus, could cross-examine not only the intertwined strands, but also the woven, crisscrossed center itself.

At the center of Brines's textual-temporal-existential weave is present time, that instant *within* which human being experiences the acts of living, remembering, projecting, loving, writing. Because human being exists *within*, what Brines terms, "el fragilísimo presente" (the very fragile present) (*SP* 41), the entire woven fabric of human existence is flimsy, delicate, weak and subject to unraveling whenever the present instant comes into being *and* ceases to be. What happens when poet and critic alike enter the labyrinthine weave of this poetry by examining closely its temporal center, the precarious present moment?

A first reading of the poem "Un olor de azahar" (A fragrance of citrus blossoms), from *El otoño de las rosas* (*OR* 20 –22), which will serve as an example, follows the thematic weave of the story of an ephemeral, amorous encounter reflecting, in essence, the transitory nature of human existence. This encounter involves a youthful, innocent "tú" (you) the "criatura que llegas bajo el sol" (creature arriving under the sun) (lines 2–3), and the older, experienced lover, the poem's first-person speaker. Knowledge of the passage of time, the transient nature of his own personal lifetime, and the fleeting act of possessing the loved one in the carnal union lead the poem's "yo" (I) first to seek (lines 3–12) and finally to attempt to possess (lines 13–20) the seemingly infinite time offered by the young lover, the

> criatura que llegas bajo el sol,
> y me ofreces el tiempo tan visible
> como tu propio cuerpo, ya desnudos
> los dos y unidos: tiempo y carne.   (lines 2–5)

> creature arriving under the sun
> and offering me time as visible

as your own body, now uncovered
the two united: time and flesh.

His effort of full possession, however, is destined to fail: "y déjame
aún tener / tu sombra entre mis manos apagada" (and permit me still to
possess / your extinguished shadow between my hands) (lines 38–39).
The poem reads as follows:

Ahora que estás tú ahí, aparecida
criatura que llegas bajo el sol,
y me ofreces el tiempo tan visible
como tu propio cuerpo, ya desnudos
los dos unidos: tiempo y carne,   5
             y ojos
que sólo están desnudos, y quisieran
ser ese tiempo, estar en esa carne,
pues busco la mentida eternidad
aún (hoy sé que todo es tiempo negro),   10
y yo soy el sumiso ante la vida
que pude imaginar, sin alcanzarla.

Te quiero amar, tocar en ti mi carne
que apagaron las noches, recobrar,
si es posible, aquel sabor gastado   15
de la vida, aquel viejo esplendor
del mar y de la luz y de mi cuerpo.

A fuerza de tenerte, y de mirarte,
que me devuelva el mundo mi mirada
y yo devolveré su luz al mundo.   20

Tocas en mí la carne que apagaron
los días, y me pides amor, quieres
acelerar tu pérdida del mundo,
saber la luz oscura de la vida,
apresar la verdad uniéndote al amado.   25

Y ahora los dos estamos en el lecho
apresurando el tiempo, en la tarde
que no es ya luz ni es sombra todavía,
             amándonos
y yendo, como siempre, cada uno   30
a ser tan sólo él.
Mas sé que has respirado junto a mí
y esta es la dicha oscura que me habita,
pues ya hubo otra ocasión que no recuerdo.

Existe otra verdad en el vacío,   35
y yo seré el vacío y la verdad,
mas no quites el aire de tus labios
de mi oído, y déjame aún tener
tu sombra entre mis manos apagada.

Cuando llegue el olvido, la memoria   40
rastreará esta dicha para nada.
Y acaso, si hay fortuna, algo recobre:
este cálido olor bajo la luna,
la primavera del naranjo blanco.

At this moment you are there, phantasmal
creature arriving under the sun,
and offering me time as visible
as your own body, now uncovered
the two united: time and flesh,   5
              and eyes
that are only uncovered, and might want
to be that time, to be in that flesh,
since I search for deceptive eternity
still (today I know that all is black time),   10
and I am resigned before the life
that I could imagine, without attaining it.
I wish to love you, to touch in you my flesh
that the nights extinguished, to regain,
if it is possible, that depleted savor   15
of life, that old splendor
of the sea and of the light and of my body.

Forcefully possessing you and gazing at you,
so that the world may return my gaze
and I shall return its light to the world.   20

You touch in me the flesh that
the days extinguished, and you ask me for love, you want
to accelerate your loss from the world,
to know the obscure light of life,
to seize the truth joining yourself to the beloved.   25

And now the two of us are in bed
hastening time, in the afternoon
that is not presently light nor shadow yet,
              loving each other
and each one going, like always,   30
to become only it.

Although I know that you have breathed next to me
and this is the obscure happiness residing in me,
as yet there was another occasion that I do not remember.

Another truth exists in the void,   35
and I shall be the void and the truth,
but don't take from my ear the breath from your lips,
and do permit me still to possess
your extinguished shadow between my hands.

When oblivion arrives, memory   40
will trace this happiness for naught.
And maybe, if there is good fortune, something may be recovered:
this warm fragrance under the moon,
the springtime of the white orange-tree.

By beginning this interrogation of the center of the Brinesean "weave
of time" with a poem written more recently, the critic already is quite
familiar with the interwoven, thematic strands of love and time in many
poems of the last three decades of his poetic production, as evident in
"Encuentro urbano" (Urban encounter) (*PE* 16 –17), "Canción de los
cuerpos" (Song of the bodies) (*IEL, ED* 231), "Trastorno en la tormen-
ta" (Upheaval in the storm) (*IEL, ED,* 230 –31), "El triunfo del amor"
(The triumph of love) (*AN, ED* 157), "El velo de amor" (The veil of love)
(*PO, ED* 109), "Tránsito de alegría" (Transition from happiness) (*PO,
ED* 111–12), "Amor en Agrigento" (Love in Agrigento) (*PO, ED*
116 –17), "Causa del amor" (Cause of love) (*PO, ED,* 124), and "Ladridos jadeantes en el césped" (Panting howls on the lawn) (*LB, ED*
24 –25), to name only a few. Had we initiated this interrogation, however, at the beginning of Brines's poetic trajectory, with a poem from
Las brasas for example, we would not have had the same temporal and
thematic perspective that we now have when studying a poem falling
into the most recent phase of Brines's poetry.[10]

By beginning at the end of Brines's poetry to date, the critic is thus
able to intertwine the temporal love story of "Un olor de azahar" with
other thematic threads of the weave of love often found in his works.
In "Un olor de azahar," in addition, a further example of human being
as a "trama del tiempo" (woof of time) (*SP* 41) is witnessed, not only
because of the temporal interlacing in the story presented but also
because of the plotline itself. In Spanish, *trama* carries not only the
meaning of weft or woof of cloth but also the additional meaning of
"plot" or "argument." In this poem the critic does witness the unfolding of actions performed by the poem's "characters," so to speak, the

two lovers. This "plot" revolves around the speaker's dual expectation of possessing fully both the loved one *and* the time belonging to the youthful "criatura" (lines 6 –9). The speaker, however, fails at both efforts because the act of love, the loved one, and the lover are merely temporal (lines 26 –31). The love story's *denouement* (in French, "unknotting"), brings together *trama* as both "woof" *and* "plot," when the speaker, in his attempt to recollect the fleeting experience of happiness in love, comes instead to comprehend: "Cuando llegue el olvido, la memoria / rastreará esta dicha para nada" (When oblivion arrives, memory / will trace this happiness for naught) (lines 40 – 41).

In looking at this first reading of the poem, we see that the speaker resigns himself to both time and love as ephemeral experiences, knowing that his resignation will forever be tempered and intensified by the return of past time and past love through memory. The act of recovery itself becomes a way to reexperience "aquel sabor gastado / de la vida" (that depleted savor / of life) (lines 15–16) just as loving the young "criatura" allows the speaker to "recobrar" (line 14), take back, that which he once possessed: his own youth now lost to the passage of time. Additionally, for this speaker, both ephemeral love and the transient present form a part of a broader cyclical view of life within time, where new love forever will be renewed and repeated: "Y acaso, si hay fortuna, algo recobre: / este cálido olor bajo la luna, / la primavera del naranjo blanco" (And maybe, if there is good fortune, something may be recovered / this warm fragrance under the moon / the springtime of the white orange-tree) (lines 42– 44).

"Un olor de azahar," however, is not a simple account of love in time, love lost to time, and the return of love in time, even if only temporarily, by means of memory. It is also, as a second reading of the poem suggests, a complex account of the time within which the speaker of the poem comprehends the (im)possibility of full possession of the present instant. In this reading, the first-person speaker possesses an ever-sensitive awareness of the present moment, an awareness that becomes more and more acute when and while the act of writing the poem takes place. *Within* that brief duration of which human being is "incessantly sensible," that instant that could be called the "conscious present,"[11] the speaker of "Un olor de azahar" participates in and questions both the coming into existence and the ceasing to be of the object of creation, the poetic text: "criatura que llegas bajo el sol, / y me ofreces el tiempo" (creature arriving under the sun / and offering me time) (lines 2–3).[12]

The simple, linear plotline of the poem's first reading becomes twisted and coiled when both the "criatura" and the time belonging to and offered by it (lines 1–3) are interrogated. *Criatura* is a "double-edged word," to borrow Johnson's term ("Introduction" xiv), whose literal meaning of "a created being or thing" could be somewhat overshadowed by the second meaning of this noun, that of "a being of very little age or of very little time", as seen in the reading of this poem offered earlier. Recalling that the Latin *creare* carries with it the notion of producing something from nothing, the "criatura" of the opening lines of "Un olor de azahar" articulates the end result of the act of creation: a created being. As such, this created object owes its being solely to its creator. This "aparecida criatura" (phantasmal creature) (lines 1–2) comes into view and displays itself before its creator in the present moment ("ahora" [at this moment] line 1), within which the act of creation takes place.[13]

The stuff, the structural material, the textual tissue ("carne," line 5) of which this created being is made is time, more specifically, the present time within which the act of writing-creating takes place (lines 3–5). For the speaker-creator of "Un olor de azahar," both the act of creating and the resultant created being incarnate present time (lines 5, 7, 13), that time which "is at hand," as the Latin root *praeesse* indicates (*DLE* 1062).[14] The poem's speaker-writer seeks possession of this time "at hand," this time that is immediately before him, this time that both is and is not his (lines 7–9). Having comprehended the temporality of his own existence, the poem's speaker-creator-writer thus seeks to possess that time belonging to his creation (lines 13–20). But why? Perhaps because, as the speaker asserts earlier in the poem, "busco la mentida eternidad / aún (hoy sé que todo es tiempo negro)" (I search for deceptive eternity / still [today I know that all is black time]) (lines 9–10). Perhaps, then, the speaker-creator looks to the present time of his created work as a way of extending his own diminishing existence: "recobrar, / si es posible, aquel sabor gastado / de la vida" (to regain, / if it is possible, that depleted savor / of life) (lines 14–16). In this way, the time of the created being becomes the time upon which the creator now depends. This form of temporal dependency undermines, however, the speaker's role as independent creator, first because this creator now owes his own being to the object he has created and secondly because instead of being adored, worshipped, loved by the created being, as most creators are, the speaker-creator wishes to love that which he has created (lines 13–20).

Perhaps the *yo*-creator-maker-poet wishes to become one with (lines 1–8; 21–25) the *tú*-created-poem. The enmeshed etymological threads of both the Latin *creare*, and its earlier Greek root *poieo* (ποιεῖν), "to make," as Moliner points out (Vol. 2, 792), tightly intertwine the text's "criatura" with the speaker-creator-writer's own act of "making" the poem.15 Perhaps, the writer hopes that greater knowledge of the present instant recorded by both poet and poem will result from their union. Images of light (lines 16 –17, 18–20) sustain this reading, since the speaker desires "saber la luz oscura de la vida, / apresar la verdad uniéndote al amado" (to know the obscure light of life, / to seize the truth joining yourself to the beloved) (lines 24 –25). What is learned, however, is only dimly known, "luz oscura," because the created being and the time it offers (lines 2–3), like the lover and the lover's own lifetime of the first reading of "Un olor de azahar" cannot be fully possessed. For the speaker-creator-writer of the poem, full possession of the present instant *within* which writing-creating takes place incessantly is both "at hand" *and* no longer "at hand" since the creator-writer is left with "tu sombra entre mis manos apagada" (your extinguished shadow between my hands) (line 39).

What is the present? The perceived, sensible instant that is immediately "at hand": now. The truth of this apparently simple definition, however, is also riddled with error because what is "at hand" *now* is also continually becoming that which is no longer "at hand." "The play of supplementarity" that, according to Harvey, "describes more precisely the structure of *différance*" (215) also describes more fully the structure of the differing and deferring present instant repeatedly created and destroyed *within* the time of the writing of "Un olor de azahar." As the present instant comes into being it also ceases to be, a temporal moment constantly added to and replaced by the past. The present is, thus, the perceived, sensible instant now "at hand" and, simultaneously, the absence of that instant. What the speaker of "Un olor de azahar" both discovers *and* questions is human being's constant experience of a "now" that is both coming into existence *and* forever ceasing to be, a "now" in which the speaker perceives the present moment ceaselessly becoming its own *différance*.16

For the speaker-creator-writer of "Un olor de azahar" this discovery and the questioning of the discovery take place *within* the act of creating-writing. When the "tú" offers the first-person speaker time (line 3), it offers "ahora" (line 1), that moment within which the creating-writing of the poem occurs. As the configuration of ink marks on the page come into being and take form in the genesis of the writing of the poem their very creation is annihilation *within* the present instant. For the speaker-writer of this poem, the act of writing exemplifies the *conscious* present, that brief, instantaneous moment of which the speaker-creator is aware. Poet-creator and poem-created object, when joined by the act of writing *within* the present moment, forever manifest, thus, not a uniquely present moment now "at hand" but rather the constant past duration of that which once was the present continually becoming "aquel sabor gastado / de la vida" (that depleted savor / of life) (lines 15–16). It is not the past that the speaker-writer tries to "recover," as at first he leads us to believe with the assertion "Te quiero amar, tocar en ti mi carne / que apagaron las noches, recobrar, / si es posible, aquel sabor gastado / de la vida." (I wish to love you, to touch in you my flesh / that the nights extinguished, to regain / if it is possible, that depleted savor / of life) (lines 13–16). On the contrary, as the act of writing takes place within present time the speaker-writer repeatedly engages in the act of recovering the present instant, ceaselessly no longer "at hand."

Once again, "the logic of the supplement," to borrow Johnson's term ("Introduction" xiii), undoes what seemed at first to be tidily arranged, contraposed thematic threads of present/past in the textual weave of "Un olor de azahar." The shadow presence of "aquel sabor gastado / de la vida" repeatedly marks the absence of "ahora" (lines 1, 26) not only in writing but also in living (lines 21–31). Returning briefly to the love story of the poem's first reading, the critic could now say that the sexual act, like the written act, incarnates the absence of the present moment. The "now" from which the immediate, sensible experience taking place *within* the present instant is constantly becoming distant is a "now" that is both present, "at hand" (*praesse*), and absent, "away" (*abesse*).[17] As the writer, however, engages in writing and joins the self to the object of creation, perhaps in subject matter ("Tocas en mí la carne que apagaron / los días" (You touch in me the flesh that / the days extinguished) (lines 21–22), or perhaps just due to the proximity of hand to pen to paper, full possession of "el fragilísimo presente" (*SP* 41) is, at once, both possible and impossible. Writing, thus, is not a way of possessing and thereby knowing the time offered by the *tú*-created object-poem, rather it is a means by which the quest(ioning) of the temporal ground of the *tú*-created object-poem takes place.

By foregrounding present time in the act of writing about and within present time the speaker-writer of "Un olor de azahar" arrives at "otra verdad en el vacío" (another truth in the void) (line 35): the present instant is a present-ceasing-to-be. The "lecho" (line 26) holding creator and created, in the poem's second reading, lover and loved one, in the poem's first reading, could be viewed figuratively as a temporary resting place. Or, if we follow the etymological branching of the Spanish noun *lecho*, from the Latin *lectus*, we find a "funeral bed, or couch or bier" (*H* 1046). The poem, then, becomes the figurative, final resting place upon which the corpse of the present moment always already lies. Further etymological retracing of this same noun takes us to yet another semantic thread in the weave of the Latin *lectus, lectum*, that of "a couch upon which it was customary to read or write" (*H* 1046).

Poet writing and poem being written manifest the fleeting, present instant each attempts to record: "Y ahora los dos estamos en el lecho / apresurando el tiempo, en la tarde / que no es ya luz ni es sombra todavía" (And now the two of us in bed / hastening time, in the afternoon / that is not presently light nor shadow yet) (lines 26–28).

The ground of the present instant is the "conflictuality of *différance*" (*POS* 44) constituting and reinscribing the past that was present, or put differently, the present endlessly becoming past. In "Un olor de azahar" the critic does not, thus, witness present in opposition to past, but rather the deconstruction of this opposition *within* the "phase of overturning" (*POS* 41). The critic not only witnesses this phase but also actively participates in it while engaged in her/his own act of critical writing, a critical writing highlighting, in itself, the present instant ceaselessly ceasing to be. The "interval between inversion" of present/past, in this poem, is marked by what Derrida describes as "the irruptive emergence of a new "concept", a concept that can no longer be, and never could be, included in the previous regime" (*POS* 42). According to Derrida, this "interval, this biface or biphase can be inscribed only in a bifurcated writing" (*POS* 42). "Un olor de azahar" manifests, then, writing that is *différance*, writing that repeatedly underscores the (in)stability of the present, writing that is a quest(ioning) of "la verdad en el vacío" (the truth in the void) (line 35).

Images of new life (lines 2; 7–16; 42–44), genesis (lines 2; 13–16; 32–33), and illumination (lines 2; 16–17; 19–20; 24; 28) abound in the poem as the speaker attempts to comprehend the created object incarnating present time. In "Un olor de azahar," as we saw in Brines's "Esplendor negro" (Black splendor) of *Insistencias en Luzbel* scrutinized in the preceding chapter, the speaker is forever seeking to comprehend the puzzles that lie before him. The quest for comprehension of the created being in "Un olor de azahar" is also a questioning of the grounds from which the quest begins each time the speaker learns that new life comes into existence and ceases to be; within genesis resides annihilation, and illumination is continuously shadowed by ignorance: "saber la luz oscura de la vida" (to know the obscure light of life) (line 24). Any advances in wisdom, thus, repeatedly take the speaker to the "verdad en el vacío / y yo seré el vacío y la verdad" (truth in the void / and I shall be the void and the truth) (lines 35–36). The speaker-creator and the poem-created being incessantly oscillate between present-past, life-death, being-nonbeing, truth-error: "Y ahora los dos estamos en el lecho / apresurando el tiempo, en la tarde / que no es ya luz ni es sombra todavía" (And now the two of us are in bed / hastening time, in the afternoon / that is not presently light nor shadow yet) (lines 26–28). Knowledge of the present moment within which creation takes place thus oscillates with ignorance of that moment whenever that moment ceases to be present while becoming past. Brines's catachrestic "tu sombra entre mis manos apagada" (your extinguished shadow between my hands) (line 39) marks the conflictual structure of opposition *and* the "interval between inversion" (*POS* 42) of that opposition: that moment in which present-past, creation-annihilation, illumination-ignorance ceaselessly are suspended.

In the final lines of "Un olor de azahar," the speaker attempts to reconcile these differences first through memory (line 40). This attempt, however, is not successful (lines 40 – 41). Both the failure of memory in time and the transient nature of the present seem to force the speaker to look beyond both the finitude of being *and* writing within the present, reaching instead an understanding of cyclical, temporal movement within nature (lines 42–44). J. Hillis Miller observes in "Ariadne's Thread: Repetition and the Narrative Line": "The end of the story is the retrospective revelation of the law of the whole. That law is an underlying 'truth' which ties all together in an inevitable sequence revealing a hitherto hidden figure in the carpet" (69).[18] In Brines's poem, this "hidden figure" in "el tejido del tiempo" takes the critic back both to the poem's title, "Un olor de azahar," and the synecdochic white blossoms of the orange-tree of the poem's final line. The poem's *denouement* leads the critic, at first, to believe that genesis, writing, being, and present time will all return in time within the cycle of existence. This unknotting of the poem's story line, however, itself becomes knotted, twisted, and tangled once again because it too occurs *within* the present instant forever not "at hand." Cyclical time, although appearing to be eternal, cannot be severed from the ephemeral, present moment (lines 15–16) to which it is inextricably bound.

"Un olor de azahar" is about present time and the play of supplementarity that is present time. This poem, then, is about both substitution and addition, where the present instant ceaselessly is replaced by the past, and the past, in turn, adds to the present the absence of the immediate instant unceasingly (not) "at hand." The present instant, thus, serves as a synecdoche, a "taking together" if we consider the Greek, for time where time is not viewed as passage, or change, or duration but rather as the incessant subversion of what is/was/will be "at hand." Synecdochic and supplemental relationships are signaled at the very beginning of Brines's poem in its very title. The noun *azahar*, from the Arabic *al-azhar* denotes "flor blanca, y por antonomasia, la del naranjo, limonero y cidro" (white flower, and through antonomasia, that of the orange, lemon and citron-trees) (*DLE* 151).[19] Antonomastically, the noun *azahar* is a naming that is a "naming instead" and it is this "naming instead," this act of nominal substitution and replacement that the critic both witnesses and in which she/he participates throughout the poem whenever "the logic of the supplement wrenches apart," to borrow Johnson's phrasing ("Introduction" xiii), the tidy opposition of present/past. The critic, like the poet, now more aware than ever of the conscious present and its fleeting contents, repeatedly witnesses a present that "names instead" the past, both throughout the poem and during her/his own critique of the poem. Like the fragrance of the aromatic citrus blossoms, the present moment is fleeting both in writing and writing about Brines's "Un olor de azahar."

As we have seen, in Brines's poetry the present moment embodies the "conflictuality of *différance*" that is time. The poems "Elca," from *Palabras a la oscuridad* (*ED* 68–69), "Elca y Montgó" (Elca and Montgó), from *Aún no* (*ED* 185–86), and "Lamento en Elca" (Lament in Elca), from *El otoño de las rosas* (*OR* 18–19), three poems from different collections in Brines's poetic production, have as their common motif the town of Elca. In "La certidumbre de la poesía," introducing *Selección propia*, Brines tells the story of Elca, explaining its significance in his poetry. This town, situated in a specific geographic local ("Es un término del campo de Oliva" [It is a district of the Olivian countryside], *SP* 50) also comes to possess specific meaning for the poet as he lives his life. Brines comments:

> En Elca transcurrió lo mejor de mi infancia, pues desde ese lugar me dispuse a contemplar con sosiego y temblor el mundo: el exterior, y el de mi cuerpo y mi espíritu. Para mí ha llegado a simbolizar el espacio del mundo. Allí lo descubrí deslumbrante y eterno, y cuando la vida me dió una visión nueva, inesperada, de mortalidad, seguí amándolo desde su pérdida, y añorando en él su antigüo e imposible engaño divino. (*SP* 50)

> In Elca I spent the better part of my childhood, in as much as from that locale I was inclined to contemplate the world with serenity and with a quiver: the external world, and that of my body and my spirit. For me it has come to symbolize the space of the world. There I discovered it dazzling and eternal, and when life presented me with a new, unexpected vision, of mortality, I continued loving it from its own loss, and mourning its ancient and impossible divine deceit.

In this story of Elca, the town becomes a personal symbol for the poet because here he came to know and to live "el sentimiento de la pérdida del mundo" (the feeling of loss from the world) (*SP* 51). Here he acquired knowledge of both his external, natural surroundings and his internal self ("en esos muros . . . asistí al lento descubrimiento de mi persona" [on these walls . . . I witnessed the slow discovery of my self] *SP* 51).

This is the story of Elca. The telling of the story of Elca, however, takes place within the poems utilizing this locale as their backdrop. Looking at these three poems in particular, "Elca," "Elca y Montgó," and "Lamento en Elca,"[20] we find what we might call successive yet differing versions of this story. How does the telling of the story of Elca in these poems about Elca differ from the story of Elca as told in the poet's prose commentary? In Brines's story about the town of his birth (*SP* 50), and in his commentary summarizing its meaning in his life, the house of his youth "está rodeada de la perenne juventud de los naranjos" (is surrounded by the perennial youth of the orange-trees) (*SP* 50). Nature incarnates and reflects the vitality of the young boy who returns summer after summer to a place where, as the poet himself states, "he vivido he gozado del mundo" (I have lived I have enjoyed the world) (*SP* 51). As the telling of this story unfolds in the heptasyllabic verses of the poem "Elca," however, we find that

> el oscuro naranjo
> ha enviudado en su flor
> para volar al viento,
> cruzar hondas alcobas,
> ir adentro del mar. (lines 21–24)

> the dark orange-tree
> has become widowed while flowering
> moving swiftly in the wind,
> crossing the deep alcoves,
> going inside the sea.

In the telling of the story of Elca in the poem "Elca," the orange-tree, a symbol of perennial youth in the story of Elca, has become "oscuro," perhaps because of the presence of the "larga sombra cae" (a long shadow falls) (line 8) in the waning afternoon, that temporal moment within which "el hombre mira el cielo / que oscurece" (the man gazes at the heavens / that darken) (lines 32–33). As day ceases to exist and as the metaphoric darkening sky shrouds the terrestrial orange-tree, the tree's flower, itself symbolic of natural vitality, exhibits, like the passing day, its own transitory essence.

The "oscuro naranjo" characterized in the telling of the story of Elca not only differs from "la perenne juventud de los naranjos" (the perennial youth of the orange-trees) of the story of Elca but also has been separated from this youthful, vital state: "el oscuro naranjo / ha enviudado en su flor" (the dark orange-tree / has become widowed while flowering) (lines 20 –21). Its blossoms are scattered by and in the wind as this tree participates in the process of living which, in this poem, is viewed as a process where vital natural and human elements come into existence *and* repeatedly cease to be: "Ya todo es flor"; "Porque todo va al mar" (Now all is flower; Because all goes to the sea) (lines 1; 7). The Spanish verb *enviudar*, to become a widower or widow, from the Latin *viduus*, bereft, void, widowed, which in turn is further linked to the Latin *dividere*, to divide (*DLE*, 547), carries within it the etymological overtones of disjunction, disunion, and dispersal. Spanish, both semantically and culturally speaking, views the widow or widower as being separated or "divided" from the conjugal partner with whom he/she had previously been joined. This disunion, marked by death, is final, for the "viuda, viudo" does not remarry. Looking at the poem, Brines's personification of "el oscuro naranjo / ha enviudado en su flor," the figurative orange-tree, has been separated from the blossoms to which it had been joined previously, and the tree's life, within nature, ceaselessly oscillates with death within time. The present perfect tense of the verb *enviudar* conveys the notion of a recently perfected action linked both to the present *and* the past, yet belonging specifically to neither. Suspended within the present instant endlessly becoming past, natural life, in the telling of the story of Elca, is both present and absent:

> Ya todo es flor: las rosas
> aroman el camino.
> Y allí pasea el aire,
> se estaciona la luz,
> y roza mi mirada   5
> la luz, la flor, el aire.
>
> Porque todo va al mar:
> larga sombra cae
> de los montes de plata,
> pisa los breves huertos,   10
> ciega los pozos, llega
> con su frío hasta el mar.
>
> Ya todo es paz: la yedra
> desborda en el tejado
> con rumor de jardín: 15
> jazmines, alas. Suben,
> por el azul del cielo,
> las ramas del ciprés.
>
> Porque todo va al mar:
> y el oscuro naranjo   20
> ha enviudado en su flor
> para volar al viento,

cruzar hondas alcobas,
ir adentro del mar.

Ya todo es feliz vida: 25
y ante el verdor del pino,
los geranios. La casa,
la blanca y silenciosa,
tiene abiertos balcones.
Dentro, vivimos todos.   30

Porque todo va al mar:
y el hombre mira el cielo
que oscurece, la tierra
que su amor reconoce,
y siente el corazón   35
latir. Camina al mar,
porque todo va al mar.

Now all is flower: the roses
perfume the road.
And there the air promenades,
the light remains stationary,
and my gaze gently touches   5
the light, the flower, the air.

Because all goes to the sea:
a long shadow falls
from the silvery mountains,
treads on the small orchards,   10
closes the wells, arrives
coldly at the sea.

Now all is peace: the ivy
overflows the roof
with the murmur of the garden: 15
jasmines, wings. Reaching upward,
through the blue sky,
the cypress branches.

Because all goes to the sea:
and the dark orange-tree   20
has become widowed while flowering
in order to move swiftly in the wind,
to cross deep alcoves,
to go inside the sea.

Now all is happy life: 25
and in the presence of the pine and its greenness,
the geraniums. The house,
white and silent,
has open balconies.
Inside, we all live(d).   30

Because all goes to the sea:
and the man gazes at the heavens
that darken, the earth
that his love recognizes,
and feels his heart   35
beating. He walks to the sea,
because all goes to the sea.

    In the telling of the story of Elca in the poem entitled "Elca" we witness not an extended, extensive process of living, as the poem's first-person speaker insistently affirms, "todo es flor" (all is flower) (line 1), "todo es paz" (all is peace) (line 13), "todo es feliz vida" (all is happy life) (line 25), but rather a ceaseless process of perpetual change *within* the present moment, that temporal instant always already ceasing to be. The poem's repeated refrain, "Porque todo va al mar" (Because all goes to the sea) (lines 7; 19; 31; 37) further underscores this process while simultaneously recalling the intertext of the famous Medieval Spanish poem *Coplas de Jorge Manrique a la muerte de su padre, el Maestre don Rodrigo* (The verses of Jorge Manrique on ·the death of his father, master don Rodrigo). Like the metaphoric "naranjo" (line 20), both natural and human life endlessly will be "widowed" from the very vitality defining them since each possesses this vitality only momentarily. The all-encompassing "todo," repeated throughout the poem, is at once viewed as a complete, full, vital whole (lines 1; 13; 25) and as a totality forever scattered *and* dispersed whenever it is joined to the spatial inmensity of the ever-changing, metaphoric sea— the source of life. Yet, like the *naranjo*, which is but a small part of this all-encompassing *todo*, the sea itself, viewed also as the symbolic goal of all life, death, simultaneously remains divided from the very vitality that it incarnates.

    The critic, by interrogating both the telling of the story of Elca, in the "Elca" poem, and its constant retelling in her/his rereading(s) of both the story and the story being told witnesses not the process of living, as the poem's opening assertion, later repeated in variation, implies ("Ya todo es flor, paz, feliz vida"), but rather the process of transition while living as the present moment becomes past. The critic, like the speaker of the "Elca" poem, remains suspended between two tem poral moments, engaged in the process of living a life that is ceasing to be. As the speaker of "Elca" observes:

> Ya todo es feliz vida:
> y ante el verdor del pino,
> los geranios. La casa,
> la blanca y silenciosa,
> tiene abiertos balcones.
> Dentro, vivimos todos. (lines 25–30)

> Now all is happy life:
> and in the presence of the pine and its greenness,
> the geraniums. The house,
> white and silent,
> has open balconies.
> Inside, we all live(d).

The verb "vivimos" (line 30), which expresses both the present tense and the preterite tense of the verb *vivir*, itself points to the precarious nature of the present, temporal moment. Both present *and* past, "vivimos" thus underscores the *différance* found *within* time, *différance* forever kept in play by the trace.

In the poem "Elca," the relentless process of present becoming past is further stressed by the adverb of time *ya* (now). Repeated three times in the poem, as the first word in the insistent affirmations "Ya todo es flor" (line 1), "Ya todo es paz" (line 13), "Ya todo es feliz vida" (line 25), its appearance both mines *and* undermines the present. *Ya* denotes, as it first meaning implies, past time in the sense of "already." Yet this past time is inextricably linked to the present moment ("es flor," "es paz," "es feliz vida" [lines 1; 13; 25]), as the second meaning of *ya* denotes. Thus, the adverb *ya*, at once refers to present time, but in relation to the past. The interconnected affirmations of "Ya todo es flor," "Ya todo es paz," "Ya todo es feliz vida" carry with them, then, the shadow presence of another state—the absence of flowers, peace and happy life which preceded these states within nature and time. Moreover, this adverb of time also carries with its expression a sense of immediacy, an immediacy rooted in present time "at this moment." Thus, right now, "todo es flor . . . paz . . . feliz vida." However, what came before? And what will it become once this present, immediate moment has ceased to be? In "Elca" the poem's speaker attempts to understand not only a particular aspect of the present moment, that brief temporal interval marking an instant that repeatedly is both coming into being *and* ceasing to be ("ya"), but also the process of becoming taking place in this temporal moment, a process repeated in the natural and human elements scrutinized throughout the poem.

In "Elca y Montgó" (Elca and Montgó), the poem's first-person speaker, while contemplating the town at the foot of the Montgó, further witnesses the present moment repeatedly differing from itself :

La tenebrosa muerte de los naranjos
deja ciego mis ojos;
anaranjada y seca, sale la luna
detrás de un mar de plomo.
Lejana, la montaña respira un aire   5
azul; la moja el mar,
en él descansa. Y así la sombra cae,
desde siglos, sobre el dolor de su dureza.
Abren los párpados las casas,
se enciende la ladera, tembloroso   10
añora el corazón seres que desconoce;
y al recuerdo regresan otros seres.

Invisible, un aire de jazmín
penetra en mi camisa, de mi carne separa
leve sudor; y este polvo soplado   15
se ha perdido en la noche,
sorda sepulturera de mi tiempo.
Fue el día piadoso,
y a la tierra gastada, agradecido,
miro con buen amor,   20
por la delicadeza con que hoy muero.

The gloomy death of the orange-trees
leaves my eyes blinded;
orange and dry, the moon appears
behind a leaden sea.
Faraway, the mountain breathes a blue air;   5
the sea dampens it,
and it rests in the sea. And thus the shadow falls,
for centuries, on the grief of its hardness.
The houses' eyelids open,
the hillside becomes inflamed, trembling   10
the heart yearns for unknown beings;
and other beings return to memory.

Invisible, a jasmine air
penetrates my shirt, removing light perspiration
from my flesh; and this blown dust   15
has become lost in the night,

the silent grave-digger of my time.
The day was pious,
and the worn out earth, grateful,
with great tenderness I watch,   20
for the gentle way in which I am dying today.

Here, the speaker's personal lifetime, metaphorically incarnated in the synecdochic "polvo" (dust) of line 15 is but itself temporal (lines 13–16). Here also, the speaker's personal lifetime is viewed as a fleeting, present moment endlessly becoming past (lines 20 –21).

The ephemeral nature of existence is captured in the metaphor "la noche, / sorda sepulturera de mi tiempo" (the night / the silent grave-digger of my time) (lines 16 –17), and the variations on this metaphor (blindness, line 2; shadow, line 6) found elsewhere in the poem. The critic might question why night plays the role of the "sepulturera."[21] Since night gradually chips away at day, especially if we view night as excavating and interring both day's light and vitality, it could be viewed then as the metaphoric tomb in which day is buried. In retracing the etymological threads of the Spanish noun *sepulturera*, the critic finds the Latin *sepulcrum* and that word's own root of *sepultus*, from *espelire*, to bury (*DLE* 1195). The metaphor, thus, seems fitting especially when night is viewed figuratively as the burial place or tomb of day.

Night in the poem's text also is depicted figuratively as the active interrer of day, an interrer who not only repeatedly engages in this act but also repeatedly has participated in this act "desde siglos" (for centuries) (line 8). Day, in turn, is depicted as the faithful witness to and participant in this event: "Fue piadoso el día" (line 18). Faithfully obedient to its own ceaseless act of becoming that which it is(not), this temporal moment, and all that it entails (luminosity, vitality, present, presence) is both undone *and* preserved by the daily, neverending ritual of becoming night and all that it entails (darkness, death, past, absence). Within this inescapable and repeated ritual, all natural and human elements daily become more and more lifeless (lines 1, 3–4, 5–7, 7–8, 13–16, 20 –21). One natural element in particular, "la montaña" (the mountain) (line 5), at first gives the appearance of stoically accepting this irreversible aspect of its own existence: "Lejana, la montaña respira un aire / azul; la moja el mar, / en él descansa" (Faraway, the mountain breathes a blue air; / the sea dampens it, / and it rests in the sea) (lines 5–7). However, when the metaphor is interrogated further, we see that acceptance has given way to a painful comprehension of nonexistence: "Y así la sombra cae, / desde siglos, sobre el dolor de su dureza" (And the shadow falls that way, / for centuries, on its hardened grief) (lines 7– 8).

One human element, the poem's first-person speaker, like the personified mountain Montgó, also comes to learn the nature of existence: "y este polvo soplado / se ha perdido en la noche, / sorda sepulturera de mi tiempo" (and this blown dust / has become lost in the night, / the silent grave-digger of my time) (lines 15–17). It is the personalized, human "mi tiempo" that is the recipient of the actions of the personified night-grave-digger. At first, it seems that the poem's speaker, like the mountain, accepts the limitations placed on the human lifetime: "agradecido, miro con buen amor, / por la delicadeza con que hoy muero" (grateful, / with great tenderness I watch, / for the gentle way in which I am dying today) (lines 20–21). However, when the critic interrogates the poem's final affirmative assertion discrepancies arise. The actions of a grave-digger are not usually considered to be "gentle" (line 21), especially if we consider the literal level of meaning associated with the noun *sepulturera*. Digging through the earth, chipping away at stone, opening sepulchers, vaults, or burial places for the dead could hardly be considered a "delicate," "gentle" undertaking. At the same time, the twists and turns in the etymological labyrinth of the noun *delicadeza* take the critic to a different meaning of the word. This noun can also denote fraility, fragility, weakness. Debilitated by his own repeated loss of life, the poem's first-person speaker, thus, forever is a witness to the ever-present finitude of his own existence. Living *within* "el fragilísimo presente," this *yo* thus lives *within* the difference that is his temporal existence. The present, like "la tierra gastada" (the worn out earth) (line 19), Montgó (lines 5–8), and the speaker's personal lifetime (lines 13–21), is inextricably linked to the state of perpetual deterioration that is existence ceasing to be. Although this daily loss of life takes place with great finesse, precision, and attention, keeping in mind both another meaning of the noun *delicadeza* and a further characterization of the actions of the figurative "noche-sepulturera," it is, nonetheless, unavoidable *within* the present moment because the "hoy" (today) within which the poem's first-person speaker lives is perpetually engaged in becoming its own *différance*.

In "Lamento en Elca" (Lament in Elca) the first-person speaker analyzes the ephemeral "momentos breves de la tarde" (brief afternoon moments) (line 1) comprising "esta breve tarde" (this brief afternoon) (line 24) within which his personal lifetime and his writing about this lifetime take place. Scrutinizing the transitory present moment in which he lives and writes, the speaker studies one specific natural element, "la luz" (the light) (line 11) *within* the present, as late afternoon fades into evening:

Estos momentos breves de la tarde,
con el vuelo de pájaros rodando en el ciprés,
o el súbito posarse en el laurel dichoso
para ver, desde allí, su mundo cotidiano,
en el que están los muros blancos de la casa,   5
un grupo espeso de naranjos,
el hombre extraño que ahora escribe.

Hay un canto de pájaros cercanos
en esta hora que cae, clara y fría,
sobre el tejado alzado de la casa.   10
Yo reposo en la luz, la recojo en mis manos,
la llevo a mis cabellos,
porque es ella la vida,
más suave que la muerte, es indecisa,
y me roza en los ojos,   15
como si acaso yo tuviera su existencia.
El mar es un misterio recogido,
lejos y azul,
                              y diminuto y mudo,
un bello compañero que te dio su alegría,   20
y no te dice adiós, pues no ha de recordarte.
Sólo los hombres aman, y aman siempre,
aun con dificultad.
¿Dónde mirar, en esta breve tarde,
y encontrar quien me mire   25
y reconozca?
Llega la noche a pasos, muy cansada,
arrastrando las sombras
desde el origen de la luz,
y así se apaga el mundo momentáneo,   30
se enciende mi conciencia.
Y miro el mundo, desde esta soledad,
le ofrezco fuego, amor,
y nada me refleja.

Nutridos de ese ardor nazcan los hombres,   35
y ante la indiferencia extraña
de cuanto les acoge,
mientan felicidad
y afirmen su inocencia,
                              pues que en su amor   40
no hay culpa y no hay destino.

These brief afternoon moments,
with the flight of birds fluttering about in the cypress,

or the sudden resting in the fortunate laurel
in order to see, from there, their everyday world,
in which the white walls of the house are,   5
a thick grouping of orange-trees,
the strange man who now writes.

There is a song from the nearby birds
in this falling hour, clear and cold,
on the raised roof of the house.   10
I rest in the light, I gather it in my hands,
I take it to my hair,
because it is life,
more delicate than death, it is indecisive,
and it rubs my eyes,   15
as if perhaps I might have its existence.
The sea is a withdrawn mystery,
faraway and blue,
                    and diminutive and silent,
a beautiful companion who gave you its happiness,   20
and does not bid you farewell, since it will not remember you.

Only men love, and they love always,
even with difficulty.
Where to look, in this brief afternoon,
and to find who may gaze at me   25
and may recognize me?
Night arrives slowly, very tired,
dragging along shadows
from the source of light,
and in this way the momentary world is extinguished,   30
my consciousness becomes inflamed.
And I gaze at the world, from this solitude,
I offer it passion, love,
and nothing reflects me.

Nurtured by that ardor men may be born,   35
and in the presence of the strange indifference
however much it protects them,
they may feign happiness
and affirm their innocence,
                              since in their love   40
there is no guilt and no fate.

The "light," which at once originates in and repeatedly vanishes within "esta hora que cae" (this falling hour) (line 9), is "indecisa" (indecisive) (line 14), suspended unsteadily between present *and* past,

afternoon *and* evening, day *and* night. The poem's speaker, continually aware of the uncertain nature of "la luz" (line 11) *within* "estos
momentos breves de la tarde" (these brief afternoon moments) (line
1), at once witnesses and experiences the fragile nature of both the act
of existing and the act of writing about existing (lines 8–16). Living
within the present and also writing *within* this temporal interval, the
poetic voice heard in "Lamento en Elca" attempts to record not only
the fleeting nature of the present moment but also the fleeting nature
of his own awareness of this present moment (lines 22–31). Both in
living and in writing about living, human being is destined to witness
endlessly the immediate, sensible, vital experience that is always ceasing to be.

The Spanish noun *conciencia* (consciousness) (line 31), from the
Latin *conscientia*, the past participle of the verb *conscire*, has at its
etymological origin *com*, a primitive form of *cum*, together with, thor-
oughly, completely, + *scire*, to know (*Etymological Dictionary of Latin*,
216). At its root, then, *conciencia* entails the possession of knowledge
as distinguished from ignorance or misunderstanding, the possession
of knowledge attained through study or practice.[22] Direct cognition
of the "mundo cotidiano" (the everyday world) (line 4) and "el mundo
momentáneo" (the momentary world) (line 30), his own vulnerable
existence within the present moment (lines 11–16, 22–31), and his
writing about his existence (line 7) within "el mundo momentáneo,"
all lead the speaker-writer of this poem to a private knowledge of the
actions in which he is presently engaged, actions repeatedly affirming the fragility of his existence within the wavering present (lines 7,
11–14, 22–26, 32–34). However, this awareness of the precarious
nature of the present, the waning afternoon, and both personal (lines
27–34) and collective (lines 22–23, 35–41) human existence constantly is undermined by the speaker's own equivocal knowledge of
all three of these states. The metaphoric "light" of illumination, wisdom, and inspiration (lines 11–16), which the speaker-writer attempts
to gather in his hands while immersed in the experience of "esta hora
que cae, clara y fría" (this falling hour, clear and cold) (line 9), is itself
"indecisa" (indecisive) (line 14). The speaker-writer of "Lamento en
Elca" forever questions the repeated and unfortunate experience of
his own finitude, the finiteness of his own writing within "estos
momentos breves de la tarde" (these brief afternoon moments) (line
1), and the fragility of the conscious present of which he writes and
in which, lamentably, he lives: "Y miro el mundo, desde la soledad,
/ le ofrezco fuego, amor, / y nada me refleja" (And I gaze at the world,
from this solitude, / I offer it passion, love, / and nothing reflects me)
(lines 32–34).

The quest for the "center" of Brines's "tejido del tiempo" takes the critic to the spurious, present moment. As we have seen in "Un olor de azahar," "Elca," "Elca y Montgó" and "Lamento en Elca," which served as examples, this single, commanding, focal point for the interlaced, temporal skein of Brines's poetry forever oscillates with the past. The present, as the deceptive center of both the "tejido del tiempo" of Brines's poetry and the "débil trama del tiempo" (weak woof of time) that is human being, is continually shadowed by the presence of the past each time the present instant comes into being and simultaneously ceases to be.

In "Está en penumbra el cuarto, lo ha invadido" (The room is in penumbra, invaded by) (*ED* 20 –21), from the 1960 collection *Las brasas*, we encounter a figure, "un bulto de sombra" (a shadowy shape) (line 4), engulfed in the tenuous light of the fading afternoon. Many of Brines's poems written throughout his poetic production take place in the penumbra, that space of partial illumination.[23] Brines often associates the penumbra with twilight, as the opening verses of the aforementioned poem reveal:

> Está en penumbra el cuarto, lo ha invadido
> la inclinación del sol, las luces rojas
> que en cristal cambian el huerto, y alguien
> que es un bulto de sombra está sentado   (lines 1–4)

> The room is in penumbra, invaded by
> the descending sun, the red lights
> that change the orchards on the window, and someone
> who is a shadowy shape is seated.

Etymological retracing of the noun *penumbra* leads the critic to the Latin *paene* "almost" and *umbra* "shadow" (*OED* 2124). The obscure protagonist of Brines's poem pertains neither to the afternoon nor the evening, the evening nor the night, but rather is situated somewhere in between these temporal moments engulfed in a light that is a half-light, a darkness that is a half-darkness. The present moment of the "bulto de sombra" (shadowy shape) is a present that is "almost" present *and* "almost" past, not specifically one or the other but rather both simultaneously. Partially present *and* partially past, the penumbra of this poem, and others in Brines's "tejido del tiempo," figuratively signals "the conflictuality of *différance*" that is the present instant ceaselessly becoming past. Ironically, the protagonist of this poem does not have to thumb through old photograph albums (lines 5–9, 13–21) in order to reexperience the past. He does not have to recollect the past through memory. Instead, his very living *within* the present instant incarnates "este rito de desmontar el tiempo" (this ritual of dismantling time) (lines 14–15).[24]

The metaphoric penumbra of this poem captures, if only momentarily, the vacillating and spurious nature of the present-center of the Brinesean "weave of time." In searching for the center of this interwoven, textual web, the critic expects, at least initially, to encounter the intertwined, temporal threads constituting that interval that she/he believes to be now existing, in progress, "at hand." The center of this weave, however, is a tangled skein where, as we have seen, the present marks *différance*.

Human being's existence *within* "el tejido del tiempo" is the material of Brines's poetry. As we have seen, the poet, through his speakers, views human being as a "weave of time"; thus in Brines's poetry we repeatedly witness a binding, a braiding of thematic, temporal and existential threads. Having first stretched and extended his figurative warp, the poet then goes to work weaving, crisscrossing from side to side, threading his way through human being's existence, which, to use Brines's own words, "sigue siendo la misma débil trama del tiempo" (continues being the same weak woof of time) (SP 41).[25] Because human being exists *within* "el fragilísimo presente," the entire woven fabric of human existence, as Brines's poetry repeatedly reveals, is "débil" (weak), subject to unraveling each time the personal, present instant comes into existence *and* ceases to be. The poet's activity of writing not only constitutes and reflects the creation of "el fragilísimo presente" but also endlessly reinscribes its ceaseless differentiation.

The critic's commentary, as we have seen, at once mimics and also extends the actions of the speakers and characters in the poems just examined. While interpreting the poetic text, the critic provides additional threads to "the woof-weave of time" that is human being, the stuff of both the poetic and the critical texts. The critic's supplemental threads themselves, however, at once manifest the (im)possibility of untangling the textual weave she/he attempts to analyze.

In the deconstructive readings of Brines's poems offered here, the present / past, beginning / end, inside / outside, union / separation division breaks down since each element of the binary opposition can only be understood in terms of the other member of the duality. Thus the critic might begin the quest for the commanding center or, perhaps, the unifying, central thread of the poetic, temporal weave that is Brines's poetry only to find, as we have seen, that she/he learns to question the very nature of the quest itself.

In this interrogation of Brines's poetry concerning time, we have seen that it is impossible not only to sort out the numerous interlaced, temporal threads but also to arrive at the center of the "tejido del tiempo" of both ephemeral human existence and poetry written about this existence. Brines's own repeated attempts throughout his poetry to untangle the "débil trama del tiempo" that is human existence point to yet additional twists and turns in the semantic snarl embedded in the Spanish noun *trama,* which can also mean *enredo,* that is, tangle, perplexity, puzzle (*Diccionario del uso,* Vol. 2, 1359). Subject to (un)raveling at any time, human being, now also viewed as a "weak tangle of time," forever traces and retraces the bypath, the footpath, the course of its own interwoven, puzzling, temporal existence, as yet another semantic thread of the Latin root *trama, trames* (*H* 1887) suggests. Living *within* "el fragilísimo presente," human being, as Brines's poems reveal, is forever acutely conscious of "el transcurso del vivir como una continuada pérdida" (the process of living as a continuous loss) (*SP* 19). Thus, both the poet's and the critic's repeated acts of (un)tangling the "weave of time" highlight the provocative and troubling query underlying all of Brines' poetry: "What is time?"

3
Differing Substitutions:
Naming "la nada"

¡Intelijencia, dame
el nombre exacto de las cosas!

Intelligence, give me
the exact name of things!   —Juan Ramón Jiménez

. . . respuestas ignorantes son todas las humanas si a la
muerte interroga.

. . . ignorant answers are all the human ones
when death is interrogated.   —Francisco Brines

Whether and how Being is must remain an open question for
the careful attention of thinking.   —Martin Heidegger

Brines has written: "al nombrar las cosas sufrimos el fascinante engaño
de su misma creación" (upon naming things we suffer the fascinating
deceit of their very creation) (*SP* 49). Through this naming-creating
the poet might hope to seek, as we saw in the preceding chapters, not
only mastery and knowledge of that which has been named-created but
also, as we shall see here, of the act of naming itself. However, Spivak
points out in the "Translator's Preface" to *Of Grammatology* that "giv-
ing a definite name is a gesture of control as authorized by metaphysical practice" (lxxi) and such a "gesture of control," as Derrida repeatedly shows, leads not to the determination of meaning and mastery of
both knowledge and language but rather to the structure of supplementarity and, importantly, the movement and play characterizing *différance*. Of *différance* Derrida observes: "It is rather because there is
no *name* for it at all, not even the name of essence or of Being, not even
that of '*différance*,' which is not a name, which is not a pure nominal

unity, and unceasingly dislocates itself in a chain of differing and deferring substitutions" (*DIF* 26).[1]

When the critic first encounters Brines's "Definición de la nada"
(Definition of nothingness) (*ED* 205), the third poem in the opening section of *Insistencias en Luzbel*, she/he might expect a precise, exact statement determinately specifying or explaining the nature of "la nada"
(nothingness), as the title seems to promise. The critic, thus, might antic-
ipate, focusing on the title of the poem, that the poetic text that follows
would offer an explanatory declaration of the meaning of the word *nada*.
It could be argued that the poem's narrative voice, in fact, does offer the
anticipated "definition" in the poem's penultimate line: "Lo pensáis
como un frío, mas esa es vuestra carne" (You imagine it to be cold, but
it is your flesh). The meaning of nonexistence is understood only by living, by being-toward the potential impossibility of existence.[2]

> No se trata de un hueco, que es carencia,
> ni del reverso de la luz;
> pues todo lo que niega constituye.
> Tampoco del silencio, que aunque es supresión,
> difunde en un sinfín naturaleza extensa.   5
> Porque hablamos desde este fiel engaño de la ficción de la palabra
> podemos enunciar esta pausa solemne:
> no se trata de la existencia cierta del concepto de Dios como Imposible.
> Ni siquiera es tampoco la previa negación de alguna insuficiencia.
>
> Lo pensáis como un frío, mas esa es vuestra carne.   10
> No afirma y nada niega su firme coherencia.

> It does not concern a hollow gap, that is an absence,
> nor the reverse of light;
> since all that it negates it constitutes.
> Neither silence, that although it is suppression,
> diffuses in an endless extensive nature.   5
> Because we speak from this faithful deceit of the fiction
>   [of the word
> we are able to enunciate this solemn pause:
> it does not concern the certain existence of the concept of God
>   [as Impossible.
> Not even is it not either the previous negation of some insufficiency.
>
> You imagine it to be cold, but it is your flesh.   10
> It does not affirm and nothing negates its firm coherence.

The critic could also argue, however, that no single declaration of
the signification of the word *nada* is forthcoming in the text. Rather,

the narrative voice offers multiple namings, determinations, explanations of "la nada": namings where sign leads to sign, where sign substitutes for sign, where sign is "under erasure," where sign reveals and conceals *différance* within the play of signification: "Porque hablamos desde este fiel engaño de la ficción de la palabra" (Because we speak from this faithful deceit of the fiction of the word) (line 6).[3] "Nada" is not "su firme coherencia" (its firm coherence) as the poem's final line asserts; rather, it has multiple and differing names, as the history of Western metaphysics, especially that of Existentialism, has shown.[4] The poem's narrative voice lists many terms used to describe, define, name "la nada:" "hueco" (hollow gap), "carencia" (absence), "reverso de la luz" (reverse of light), "silencio" (silence), "el concepto de Dios como Imposible" (the concept of God as Impossible), "negación de alguna insuficiencia" (negation of some insufficiency), "frío" (cold), "vuestra carne" (your flesh) (lines 1–10). However, the speaker quickly points out, in the act of defining "la nada" in terms of the clichéd expressions previously used to name this notion, that "la nada" also does not go by these names. One sign may be substituted for another, but the substitution is never exact: "No se trata de un hueco" (It does not concern a hollow gap) (line 1); "ni del reverso de la luz" (nor the reverse of light" (line 2); "Tampoco del silencio" (Neither silence) (line 4); "no se trata de la existencia cierta del concepto de Dios como Imposible" (It does not concern the certain existence of the concept of God as Impossible) (line 8); "Ni siquiera es tampoco la previa negación de alguna insuficiencia" (Not even is it not either the previous negation of some insufficiency) (line 9). The sign is "a structure of difference," to borrow Spivak's observation (xvii), and in Brines's "Definition of nothingness" the critic's tracing and retracing of the sign throughout the text only leads to its ubiquitous undecidability.

"Definición de la nada" could be viewed, keeping in mind the Latin *definire* (*H* 531), as an attempt to bring to an end, to settle the limits of, to limit the existential mode of "la nada" by stating determinately its essential nature.[5] Both the poem and the ontological concept, however, despite the poem's title, function against this act of defining, explaining, declaring the signification of "la nada," or put differently, of bringing to an end any semantic ambiguity that might possibly be associated with the term. The starting point of the poem, the title, is incompatible with the plurality of definitions that follow. Not only does "la nada" have many other namings but also such namings clarify as they obfuscate, reveal as they conceal the declaration of the signification of this concept. It seems that "la nada" both neatly points to a single determination such as "hueco" (hollow gap) (line 1) yet at the same time stubbornly refuses this single semantic substitution: "No se trata de un hueco, que es carencia" (It does not concern a hollow gap, that is an absence) (line 1).

The text goes about this act of (under)mining signification in a few different ways. The rhetorical device of ellipsis could be viewed as an extension of the conceptual ellipsis involved in the notion of "nothingness": omission, lack, absence. The absence of the syntactic subject "la nada" in lines 1, 3, 4, 8, 9, and 11, compounded with the omission of the verbal phrase "se trata de" in lines 2 and 4, stylistically call attention to nonbeing, the notion that is being defined.[6] However, the use of ellipsis, a "leaving out" in Greek, simultaneously underscores both the absence *and* the presence of the word or the phrase omitted, an absence *and* presence already signaled by the concept of nonexistence. Retracing the seemingly parallel syntactic constructions of "se trata de" + object in lines 1, 2, 4, and 8 might lead the critic to believe that the syntactic objects of this verbal construction, "hueco" (line 1), "reverso de la luz" (line 2), "silencio" (line 4) and "la existencia cierta del concepto de Dios como Imposible" (line 8), are equivalents. Rather than moving closer and closer to a single meaning of "la nada," as the critic might have anticipated at the beginning of the progression of these supposedly equivalent and substitutive namings, she/he really has moved further and further away from a determinate "meaning" for and a singular definition of "la nada." This play and interplay of substitutions for "la nada" point to the endless movement of *différance* within the language of naming throughout the text. As Derrida points out in *Positions*, "*différance* finds itself enmeshed in the work that pulls it through a chain of other 'concepts', other 'words', other textual configurations" (*POS* 40). Although it seems, at first, that a transcendental signifier and signified have been privileged, given the poem's title, no such privileging is possible since the "conflictuality of *différance*" (*POS* 44), evidenced in naming, prevents a singular, definitive "Definition of nothingness."

It is not that "la nada" "means" nothing, nothingness, nonbeing, nonexistence, absence, emptiness of concept, indeterminate notion of being, explanations that the *Dictionary of Philosophy* might offer, or "hollow gap," "reverse of light," "silence," "cold," explanations offered in Brines's "Definición de la nada," or "ese dios Hueco" (that Hollow god), a naming found in Brines's "Tríptico de la aventura" (Triptych of the adventure) (line 12, *OR* 97), or "(yo que no soy)" (I who am not) found in his "El ojo solitario de la noche" (The solitary eye of the night) (line 18, *OR* 111), or "vacío" (void) encountered in his poems "Reminiscencias" (*AN, ED* 188– 89) and "El sueño desde la nada" (The dream from nothingness) (*OR* 110), to name but a few other namings encountered in this "supplementary series" (*OG* 183) of namings in Brines's poetry. Rather, "la nada" "means" everything that is/has been associated with such substitutions, now viewed as replacements, and also everything not associated with such substitutions, simultaneously viewed as displacements.[7] It is not that "la nada" has a single name, a single definition, and thus can be known only by this single name and single definition. Rather, as the critic moves along "the course of the supplementary series" (*OG* 184) she/he sees that "la nada" has many names, many representations, many inexact substitutions—each of which is repeatedly dislocated by "supplementary *différance*" (*OG* 183). It is not that language is insufficient or, as Persin argues, "the poet's efforts to describe that experience [the void] are found to be lacking" (*RSP* 50).[8] On the contrary, the sign always already is a structure of perpetual difference *and* deferral.

In Brines's poem, then, the failure to determine "la nada" within a singular "definition" of this abstract notion demonstrates not the explanatory boundaries or semantic limitations promised by the title, "Definition of nothingness," but rather the expanding nature and play of signification bound up in the chain of differing and deferring substitutions now constituting and reconstituting this "definition." Instead of setting the limits of "la nada," as the Latin *definire* denotes (*H* 531), the text presents a series of differing namings and differing significations for this ontological concept. Boundaries on the "meaning" of "la nada" are not established here, nor are they precisely designated with exact namings; rather, the concept is expanded by *différance*. The naming and renaming, the imaging and reimaging of "la nada," in "Definición de la nada" and throughout *Insistencias en Luzbel*, lead to the quest(ioning) of the unity of language itself. This act also leads to textuality and the expansion of the entire notion of metaphoricity.[9] Defining "la nada" is at once both a possible and an impossible task not because of the limits of language but rather because of the limitless chain of differing and deferring substitutions used in the naming and renaming of this concept. As Brines writes in the opening poem of *Insistencias en Luzbel*, "Esplendor negro" (Black splendor), studied in chapter 1: "las palabras son tan sólo expresión de un engaño" (words are only the expression of a deceit) (line 14, *ED* 203), or put differently in "Definición de la nada:" "hablamos desde este fiel engaño de la ficción de la palabra" (we speak from that faithful deceit of the fiction of the word) (line 6, *ED* 205). When using language, while writing about and while attempting to define "la nada," the familiar becomes unfamiliar and the unfamiliar becomes familiar as the critic traces and retraces "la nada," as the critic charts the tracks of the movement of *différance*, as the critic follows the twists and turns, the signs and the detours of the language used in writing both the poetic and the critical texts.

Returning briefly to the poem's title, the critic, as we have seen, initially expects a direct attempt, on the part of the poem's narrative voice, a direct statement defining and naming "la nada." She/he, thus, begins reading the poem anticipating, even believing, that something—in this case "nothing"—will be explained. The critic first encounters and then follows a series of assertions involving a series of negative declarations of what "la nada" is not, assertions that might lead her/him to believe that ultimately, perhaps in the poem's closing lines, a positive definition will be forthcoming and the formerly vague notion "la nada" will finally be given an exact meaning and will be defined once and for all. The poem's repeated and seemingly straightforward syntactical pattern "no se trata de" (lines 1, 2, 4, 8) heightens the critic's expectation of the possible, forthcoming, positive explanation of what "la nada" might be given the previous statements of what it is not. However, no such positive definition comes about and thus the critic's expectation is left unfulfilled. Instead, the critic confronts the poem's final line: "No afirma y nada niega su firme coherencia" (It does not affirm and nothing negates its firm coherence) (line 11). Here, the closing assertion is itself a negative declaration implying both the truth and the error of the statement being made. This closing assertion is undermined not only by the presence of "no" ("no afirma") but also by the absence of an explicitly stated subject for the verb *afirma*. If the subject of the verb *afirma* is "la nada," then it is "nothingness" that neither affirms nor negates. So what, then, does "nothingness" do if it "neither affirms nor negates?" It seems that this closing assertion creates merely the illusion of knowledge of what "la nada" is. Doubt further shadows the poem's closing statement in yet another way. "Su firme coherencia" (its firm coherence) could function as the syntactic subject and/or object of the verb *niega*.[10] The poem's own assertions continually defer their own differing, referential effects, their own difference. The attempted explication of "la nada" offered both in the poetic text and the critical commentary on that text ceaselessly trace and retrace the movement of *différance*, a movement where, as Harvey explains, "*différance* . . . is (a) precisely what it claims it is not, yet also (b) is not precisely that which it claims to be" (243). In "Definición de la nada," the very act of defining "la nada" exposes the presence-absence of a logocentric "coherencia" upon which its definitions may have been based or could be based. There is no structural unity ("firme coherencia"), however, in either the act of naming or the name "la nada; there is only *différance*.

Brines's preoccupation with naming "la nada" does not begin nor does it end with *Insistencias en Luzbel*. Rather, it is a constant concern expressed both in his poetry and his prose commentaries on his poetry. In *Las brasas* and *Palabras a la oscuridad*, his earliest works, "la nada" has other names that are further substitutions, corrections, replacements and displacements all naming, despite their different names, the "same" thing. In "El balcón da al jardín . . ." (The balcony opens to the garden) (*ED* 19), the opening poem of the first section of *Las brasas*, "la nada" is named directly as "muerte" (death), and indirectly or figuratively as "una sombra fría" (a cold shadow), "un aliento poderoso" (a powerful breath) (lines 21–23). In "Junto a la mesa se ha quedado solo" (He has remained alone near the table) (*ED* 23–24), the motif of the penumbra names indeterminate existence ceasing to be. The speaker's focus is not on the end result of death but rather on the process of dying while living: "Ay, se muere todo, / pasa la luz, la flor, los sentimientos / se marchitan, las fuerzas van perdiéndose" (Alas, all dies, / light fades, the flower, emotions / wither, strength constantly is slipping away) (lines 20 –22). In "Está en penumbra el cuarto, lo ha invadido" (The room is in penumbra, invaded by) (*ED* 20 –21), the metaphoric motif of the trip underscores living toward ultimate death. Here, death is described as an "island" of which the aging protagonist dreams (lines 31–34), and where one day he will come to rest after completing his journey of life: "Un día partirá del viejo pueblo / y en un extraño buque, sin pesar, navegará" (One day he will depart from his old town / and in a strange boat, weightless, he will navigate) (lines 35–37). On the part of the aging protagonist of this poem, and others in Brines's poetic production, knowledge of death results in the stoic acceptance of the process of living toward the inevitable finitude of being. His early poems thus demonstrate a use of traditional metaphoric namings for nonexistence, where death not only marks but also "names" the natural and inescapable terminus of life.

In both *Las brasas* and *Palabras a la oscuridad*, however, we are far from the urgent questioning of "la nada" encountered in "Definición de la nada." Brines's early poems examining nonexistence tend to view this existential mode from a personal perspective where "los signos de la muerte" (the signs of death) (line 33, "Los signos desvelados" [The vigilant signs] *PO, ED* 78) are inextricably linked to human life: "Sentado aquí, repito / la vida de otros muertos" (Seated here, I repeat / the life of the dead) (lines 21–22, "Plaza en Venecia" [Venetian plaza], *PO, ED* 79). Images of night, darkness, shadow, and fading light pervade *Palabras a la oscuridad*, for example, as the various poetic speakers attempt to investigate and come to terms with "la inquietud misteriosa / de las cosas que mueren" (the mysterious restlessness / of dying things) (lines 46 – 47, "Escrito en el humo" [Written in smoke] *ED* 139). Nonexistence, named "la muerte" (the death), is both the enigma ("Entra el pensamiento en la noche" (Thought enters the night) (*ED* 65– 68) and the inevitable, ubiquitous "ley fatal del mundo" (fatal law

of the world) (line 35, "Otoño inglés" [English autumn], *ED* 106).
Knowledge of the possibility of nonexistence leads many speakers in
this 1966 volume to take consolation in the continuance of natural life
after personal existence has ceased ("Isla de piedras" [Island of stones],
ED 97–98). Other poetic voices, however, reveal a more cynical attitude toward the finitude of human existence, a cynicism that will inten-
sify in *Aún no* and *Insistencias en Luzbel*. In "Ceniza en Oxford" (Ashes
from Oxford) from *Palabras a la oscuridad*, for example, the poem's
aging first-person speaker contemplates the youth of others "mientras
mi voz os suena funeral" (while my voice sounds funereal to you) (line
8). Fully aware of his own mortality, the speaker questions the validity and purpose of nonexistence: "(Tan sólo un podersoso cadáver que
soñara / nos pudiera crear de esta manera)" (Only a powerful dreaming
corpse / might be able to create us in this way) (lines 17–18, *ED* 103).
In "Muerte de un perro" (Death of a dog) (*ED* 144 – 45), "la muerte" is
named directly when the first-person speaker witnesses the brutal and
senseless action of young boys killing a dog and the effect of this on the
vulnerable animal: "porque la muerte le obligaba, con su prisa ira-
cunda / a desertar de dentro tanta sustancia por vivir" (because death
obligated him, with its enraged haste / to abandon from within such sub-
stance by living) (lines 13–14). This effect is intensified when "la
muerte" is renamed "vacío" (void) when the poem's speaker personal-
ly identifies with the dog's ultimate extinction and the resultant "terror al vacío" (terror before the void) (lines 18–24).

In *Aún no*, the poems' numerous speakers confront and question
more directly "el fracaso de la vida" (the ruin of life) (line 21, "Mendigo de realidad" [Beggar of reality], *ED* 156). Life is no longer viewed
as a transitional phase, as it was in *Las brasas*, for example, nor is it
viewed as an undecipherable mystery, as it was in *Palabras a la oscuridad*. In *Aún no* various speakers, having learned by living that being is
spurious, interrogate "el sueño roto de la vida" (the broken dream of
life) (line 13, "Cuando yo aún soy la vida" [When I still am life], *ED*
198). This multifaceted interrogation involves an inquiry into mortality and immortality, life and death, the ephemeral and the eternal
reflected in the poem "Alocución pagana" (Pagan allocution) (*ED*
164 – 65), which serves as an example:

> ¿Es que, acaso, estimáis que por creer
> en la inmortalidad,
> os tendrá que ser dada?
> Es obra de la fe, del egoísmo
> o de la desolación.   5
> Y si existe, no importa no haber creído en ella:

respuestas ignorantes son todas las humanas
si a la muerte interroga.

Seguid con vuestros ritos fastuosos, ofrendas a los dioses
o grandes monumentos funerarios,   10
las cálidas plegarias, vuestra esperanza ciega.
O aceptad el vacío que vendrá,
en donde ni siquiera soplará un viento estéril.
Lo que habrá de venir será de todos,
pues no hay merecimiento en el nacer   15
y nada justifica nuestra muerte.

Is it that, perhaps, in your opinion by believing
in immortality,
it will have to be given to you?
It is an act of faith, egoism,
or desolation.   5
And if it exists, it is not important not having believed in it:
ignorant answers are all the human ones
when death is interrogated.

Continue with your pompous rites, offerings to the gods
or famous funereal monuments,   10
the burning supplications, your blind hope.
Or accept the void that will come,
where not even a sterile breeze will blow.
What will have to come about will be for all,
since there is no merit in being born   15
and nothing justifies our death.

It is in *Insistencias en Luzbel* and *El otoño de las rosas*, however, where Brines's interrogation of the spurious nature of being is most fully developed. The existentialist terminology already evident in *Aún no*, with such namings and renamings as "vacío" (void) ("El triunfo del amor" [The triumph of love], ED 157), "Reminiscencias" (Reminiscences) (ED 188–89), "La última estación de los sentidos" (The last season of the senses) (ED 194–95), "hueco sofocante" (suffocating hollow gap) ("Sombrío ardor" [Somber ardor], ED 162), and "nada" (nothingness) ("Epitafio romano" [Roman epitaph], ED 164), to mention a few, becomes more insistent in *Insistencias en Luzbel*, in particular. "Definición de la nada," examined earlier, could be viewed as a compendium of many of the namings used previously, by both Brines and by other existentialists, in order to describe "la nada." However, as we saw earlier, this poem is more than just one more attempt at naming "non-existence." The poet's own interrogation, through his poetic speaker, of the notion of nonbeing, lead the poet, the speaker, and ultimately the critic to question the very language employed in the written interrogation. Namings and renamings, corrections and added corrections, substitutions and displacements only serve to mark the instability, fragility, and heterogeneity of the sign and the unceasing movement of *différance*.[11]

Derrida has shown us that the subject repeatedly is decentered in writing, with every movement of the pen, with every chain of substitution, with every addition, replacement, displacement of sign for sign, of signifier and signified. Harvey explains this decentering in this way: "the play of *différance* at once constitutes the context of a term and therein its meaning, and also shifts that same context so as to therein already alter and defer meaning as such" (240). In Brines's poetry of the last thirty years, each time "la nada" is named it is also unnamed only to be named, renamed then unnamed again and again with, in, and by means of the proliferation of the differing, supplemental namings for "la nada." Such namings repeatedly call attention to writing as the play of *différance*, writing as a chain of differing and deferring substitutions, writing as the disruption of knowing through and by means of naming, writing as the redoubling and repetition of differences.[12]

In Brines's "Definición de la nada" difference is a strategy of writing and of reading. This strategy also comes into play in other poems from the same collection. In "Desde el error" (From the error) (*ED* 209), for example, the poem's speaker offers a critique of language within and while using language. The sign does not name exactly; rather, writing clarifies and obfuscates the story of the truth-error of existence and the story of the truth-error of writing about existence featured throughout *Insistencias en Luzbel*.[13] In the poem "Los sinónimos" (The synonyms) (*ED* 212), to cite a further example, the critic witnesses yet another attempt at naming "la nada" by means of successive, inexact, displaced substitutions that point to the instability of the sign:

> Más allá de la luz está la sombra,
> y detrás de la sombra no habrá luz
> ni sombra. Ni sonidos, ni silencio.
> Llámele eternidad, o Dios, o infierno.
> O no le llames nada.
> Como si nada hubiera sucedido.

> Beyond the light is the shadow,
> and behind the shadow there will not be light
> nor shadow. Nor sounds, nor silence.
> Call it eternity, or God, or hell.
> Or call it nothing at all.
> As if nothing had taken place.

Here, the more precisely the poem's narrative voice aims at clarifying by means of naming, the less clear both the naming and the name become. To name is to distinguish, yet appellation in "Los sinónimos," despite the title, leads to a multiplicity of the name, the named, and the naming. The critic does not arrive at the same meaning, as both the Latin and the Greek roots of the Spanish *sinónimo* imply. Rather, the critic encounters the very inscription and condition of difference and deferral within the act of naming. Derrida observes: "There was in fact a first violence to be named. To name, to give names that it will on occasion be forbidden to pronounce, such is the originary violence of language which consists in inscribing within a difference, in classifying, in suspending the vocative absolute" (*OG* 112). This "inscribing within a difference" is the insistent mode of writing, the insistent "play of signifying references, that constitute language" (*OG* 7) found throughout and exploited within Brines's *Insistencias en Luzbel*. Thus, despite the title of one poem of the collection, no "Significación última" (Final meaning) (*ED* 211) is ever forthcoming for "el vacío" (the void), "la muerte" (the death), "el secreto fiel" (the faithful secret) (lines 3, 8, 9); rather, there is only differentiation in naming.

In *Insistencias en Luzbel* the critic repeatedly witnesses "la nada" appearing as the *différance* (difference-deferment) of "el olvido" (forgetfulness': "¿Qué es más (o menos): la nada o el olvido? / La nada: un imposible; / el olvido: un misterio" (What is more (or less): nothingness or forgetfulness? / Nothingness: an impossibility; / forgetfulness: a mystery) ("Desde el error" [From the error], lines 1–3 *ED* 209) Put differently: "Creamos el olvido, pues manchamos la nada" (We create forgetfulness, then we stain nothingness) ("Desde el error," line 12). Again put differently: "Cuando deseamos la nada, estamos inventando el olvido" (When we desire nothingness, we are inventing forgetfulness) ("Identificación en el espejo" [Identification in the mirror], line 11, *ED* 212). While living, whenever "la nada" differs with and defers to "el olvido" does not human being display its own desire to "forget" this ontologicial possibility? Does not this nominal substitution signal, perhaps, that because human being, in attempting to name, to designate nonexistence, comes to name instead its own desire to "forget" inevitable human finitude?[14] Throughout *Insistencias en Luzbel*, it seems, whenever the speakers attempt to name exactly "la nada" this naming points to differing namings that continuously expand this notion. This substitutive play occurs often in *Insistencias en Luzbel* where sign is replaced and displaced by sign, where sign is ceaselessly placed "under erasure."[15] We find, for example, in "Mis dos realidades" (My two realities) (*ED* 216): "Era un pequeño dios: nací inmortal" (line 1) (I was a little god: I was born immortal) (line 1), and later in the poem "Miradme ahora mortal; sólo culpable" (Look at me now mortal; only culpable) (line 18). This questioning of mortality is repeated in the opening epigraph to the second section of the volume of poems, "Insistencias en el engaño" (Insistences on deceit) (*ED* 213):

> Nacimos inocentes; hoy, culpables.
> Qué significa el tiempo? Devastados.
> Nacemos inmortales; hoy, mortales.
> El nombre de la vida es el Engaño.

> We were born innocent; today culpable.
> What is the meaning of time? We are devastated.
> We are born immortal; today, mortal.
> The name of life is Deceit.

Throughout *Insistencias en Luzbel* the dilemma underlying human existence is highlighted repeatedly by the supplemental play of the sign marking a place of difference and deferment.

The chain of differing and deferred substitutions throughout this collection of poetry marks not only the structure of *différance* but also points to writing as "the supplement par excellence." Derrida reminds us:

> If supplementarity is a necessarily indefinite process, writing is the supplement par excellence since it proposes itself as supplement of supplement, sign of sign, *taking the place of* a speech already significant it displaces the *proper place* of the sentence, the unique time of the sentence pronounced *hic et nunc* by an irreplaceable subject, and in turn enervates the voice. It marks the place of the initial doubling. (*OG* 281)

Such supplemental writing inscribes and reinscribes the various "insistences" of *Insistencias en Luzbel*, especially when the numerous poetic voices scrutinize carefully the notion of human mortality and attempt to name precisely this mode of being. In "El extraño habitual" (The habitual stranger), for example, the poem's speaker affirms: "La casa . . . Aquí descubrió el mundo; lugar para morir" (The house . . . Here he discovered the world; a place to die) (lines 1, 4, *ED* 219). Within this differing chain of appellative substitutions we also find " 'Soy misterioso: sufro, y no me quedo' " (I am mysterious: I suffer, and I do not remain) ("Epitafio del vivo" [Epitaph of the living], line 1, *ED* 223), which is further re-imaged as "Hemos quemado muchos cigarrillos, / y así se fue la vida" (We have smoked many cigarettes, / and that is how life slipped away) ("Resumen fantástico" [Fantastic summary], lines 1–2, *ED* 227), which is also further re-presented as "El nombre de la

vida es el Engaño" (The name of life is Deceit) (*ED* 213), which is further re-figured as "en vez de Dios o el mundo / aquel Esplendor negro"
(instead of God or the world / that black Splendor) ("Esplendor negro"
[Black splendor] lines 9–10, *ED* 203), which is also redefined as "Lo
pensáis como un frío, mas esa es vuestra carne" (You imagined it to be
cold, but it is your flesh) ("Definición de la nada" [Definition of noth-
ingness] line 10, *ED* 205), and the namings and renamings continue
throughout Brines's poetry. Writing, in *Insistencias en Luzbel*, continues to display the play of supplemental signification, because, as Harvey tells us, writing "is never full, yet always too full and overflowing
its own bounds" (150). In *Insistencias en Luzbel*, the critic, thus, repeatedly encounters differing and deferring appeals insistently subverting
the stability of the sign.

This chain of differing substitutions in *Insistencias en Luzbel* is further
evident in the epigraph entitled "Luzbel" (*ED* 203):

> Descifremos el mito:
> el Angel es la nada;
> Dios, el engaño.
> Luzbel es el olvido.

> Let us decipher the myth:
> the Angel is nothingness;
> God, deceit.
> Lucifer is forgetfulness.

This brief, introductory poem establishes a series of identity equations
where "El Angel" (The Angel) is replaced and also displaced by "la
nada" (nothingness), "Dios" (God) by "el engaño" (deceit), and "Luzbel" (Lucifer) by "el olvido" (forgetfulness). The acts of naming and
renaming at work in the poetic texts of the collection are foreshadowed
and sustained by the series of epigraphs interspersed throughout part
one of *Insistencias en Luzbel* and introducing part two of this same
work. The poetic texts of parts one and two furnish additional designations, repeated and extended appellative substitutions charting the
movement of *différance*.

Interrogating this opening "myth," an angel is considered to be a
celestial being acting as the agent, messenger or envoy of God, especially if we review Christian tradition. Additionally, an angel
possesses infinite being.[16] Yet in the epigraphic "Luzbel" poem,
which inscribes the "myth" of *Insistencias en Luzbel*, "El Angel" is
equated with "la nada," that which is devoid of being. If this figu-

rative and enigmatic emissary is carrying a message, what is in this message? And to whom is it to be delivered? And for what purpose? Does this message, perhaps, concern the finitude of being, as "la nada" denotes? Is this message as empty as the "nothingness" with which its carrier has been equated? An angel, at least in Christian lore, commonly is viewed as an intermediary between God and humankind. The "God" described in this epigraph, however, is equated with "el engaño" (deceit). Could the communication carried by the messenger manifest, then, the "deceit" characterizing the communicator?

Christian theology has shown us that when the human being posits the existence of God, human being is then liberated from personal, ultimate finitude due to the possibility of the life everlasting offered by God. In Christian theology, God thus represents both salvation from death and the extension of life. Returning to Brines's epigraphic poem, within his myth of existence, "God" is replaced by another naming, that of "deceit," and thus the possibility of eternal life is now viewed as doubtful, jeopardized by the "engaño" now associated with the Supreme Being. A differing naming thus displaces all that normally has been associated with the appellation "Dios." This particularized act of naming, *Dios-engaño*, is not, however, a singular, determinant designation. Rather, it is complicated even further by the opening epigraph of the second section of the collection when the narrative voice proclaims: "El nombre de la vida es el Engaño" (The name of life is Deceit) (*ED* 213). The initial *Dios-engaño* nominal substitution now has been designated differently once more as the naming *vida-engaño* both adds to *and* replaces the differing and equivocal identity of "Dios."

If both "God" and "life" are "deceit" what, then, remains for humankind? Returning to the introductory, epigraphic "myth," perhaps human being needs "to forget" the possibility of impending non-existence, instead opting to succumb to the temptations of "Luzbel:" "Luzbel es el olvido" (Lucifer is forgetfulness). Since death can no longer be suspended because God now is viewed as "deceit," perhaps this Brinesean myth of existence is urging, then, that human being "forget" death and listen, instead, to the many insistent temptations life might offer.[17] Many of the poems in the second section of *Insistencias en Luzbel*, entitled "Insistencias en el engaño" (Insistences on deceit), seem to argue just this. Knowledge of death on the part of many of these speakers gives to life a sense of urgency that it might otherwise not have—urgency to pursue what one speaker calls "Los placeres inferiores" (The inferior pleasures) (*ED* 229–30), urgency to participate fully in the pursuit and enjoyment of carnal pleasure. Life has this sense of urgency because it is, as the epigraph introducing the second section of the collection discloses, "el engaño." Life, thus, is not infinite nor does life suspend the possibility of death infinitely; rather, life relentlessly moves towards its own terminus.

Past critical commentary on *Insistencias en Luzbel* often has viewed the figure of "Luzbel" as an equivalent denomination for Satan, "the god of darkness," whose name, as Persin points out, reveals a paradox: "the light-bearer as the Prince of Darkness" (*RSP* 46). Commenting on the epigraphic poem "Luzbel," Persin observes:

> In using the first-person plural imperative of the verb *descifrar*, the poet-speaker invites the reader to join him in his interpretation of the myth of existence. The specific spiritual reality of *Dios, el Angel,* and *Luzbel* is juxtaposed and identified with that of absence, in the form of *nada, engaño,* and *olvido.* In parallel fashion, on a metapoetic level, the poet must confront the subversive component of language, namely, that language is a set of empty forms. Thus the poet wishes to call into question language's power to communicate. Nothingness, illusion and the the void of 'un-memory' are the poet's tools of deciphering and describing human destiny. (*RSP* 48)

Bradford offers this added observation regarding this collection of poems:

> The first part of *Insistencias en Luzbel* . . . concerns the Fall. The story of Lucifer serves as a point of departure for the development of rational premises that decode myth and substitute in its place a poetic dialectic of nothingness. In this later work Brines is not so stoically resigned to his fate as in earlier works, and there is a rebellion against death in which the poet identifies with Lucifer. For Brines, Lucifer's rebellion against God and his battle with the Angel symbolize modern man's rebellion against an absurd world. ("Dialectic" 1–2).

Debicki adds another supplementary explication of this 1977 collection when he writes:

> External reality now appears totally transformed to fit the subjective vision of the poet, and serves as the correlative of a negative yet rebellious outlook on life and art. The story of Lucifer is the basis for a whole new myth of existence: In the first part of the book ("Insistencias en Luzbel") Lucifer's rebellion is a sign of modern man's existential battle against a meaningless and time-limited existence. The second part ("Insistencias en el engaño") is more heterogenous, reflecting various aspects of man's efforts to affirm himself within an absurd world by means of love, sex, and poetry. (*PD* 36)

Brines himself furnishes yet an additional interpretation of the epigraphic poems of *Insistencias en Luzbel* when he comments:

> En la lectura de los primeros términos . . . se formula el mito, aquí metafóri-
> co, del Angel caído: quiso ser Dios, y fue condenado. En la de los segundos
> el mito es el mío personal, creado desde la poesía: la Nada como posibilidad
> frustrada, y que al transformarse en Ser, en Vida, es condenada al Olvido. El
> Olvido es la nada manchada por la vida. El proceso a que aboca hace que
> llame, a la Vida, Engaño. Luzbel es, pues, en la metáfora, el término que se
> corresponde con el Olvido.[18]

> In the reading of the first terms . . . the myth is formulated, here metaphor-
> ically, of the fallen Angel: he wanted to be God, and he was condemned. In
> that of the second the myth is more personal, created from the poetry: Noth-
> ingness as a frustrated possibility, and that upon being transformed into Being,
> into Life, is condemned to Forgetfulness. Forgetfulness is nothingness stained
> by life. The process has him call Life, Deceit. Lucifer is, then, in the
> metaphor, the term to which Forgetfulness corresponds.

These multiple readings of the metaphoric figure of "Luzbel" of *Insistencias en Luzbel* can all be viewed as different quests in search of the
structure that will reduce discrepancies to a single interpretation, thus
highlighting and identifying a consistent, stable, meaningful center
both for the metonymic figure of "Luzbel" and the poems in the collection bearing his name.[19]

What happens, however, when the differential and referential aspects
of the name "Luzbel" are interrogated? What happens when differences are not reduced but rather allowed to come into play? What happens when sign, signifier and signified differ? The Spanish noun *luzbel* is derived from the Latin *lucifer* (*DCE*, Vol. 2, 718). The Latin
lucifer, from *lux-fero*, can be defined as "light-bringing" (*H* 1080).
Within the twists and turns of the semantic substitutions occurring in
the etymological retracing of the Latin *lucifer*, we find namings such as
"the morning star, the planet Venus" (*H* 1080), when it appears in the
sky before sunrise, and the "day-star" (*OED* 1674). The arbitrary
nature of the word *lucifer* also is exposed in its very use. *A Dictionary
of Angels* tells us that *lucifer* ("light giver") has been "erroneously
equated with the fallen angel (Satan) due to a misreading of Isaiah
14:12: 'How art thou fallen from heaven, O Lucifer, son of the morning', an apostrophe which applied to Nebuchadnezzar, king of Babylon" (176).[20]*A Dictionary of the Bible* notes of the term *lucifer* that "The
word is applied by the writer of the prophecy [Is 14:12] to the king of
Babylon, partly in reference to the astrology for which Chaldea was
famous in ancient times, partly to the prevailing belief in the deifica-
tion of heroes" (159). Explaining further:

> The king of Babylon had complacently looked forward to the time when he
> would ascend into heaven and exalt his throne above the stars of God. But in

reality his dead body would be treated with the utmost contempt, (a carcase trodden under foot); while his soul would descend into Sheol, and there receive but an empty honour from the shades, astounded that the great and the mighty king could become like one of themselves.

From a supposed reference to this passage in our Lord's words, 'I beheld Satan fallen as lightning from heaven' (Lk 10:18), in connexion with Rev 9: 1–11 (the language of 9: 1 being in part probably derived from this passage), Lucifer came in the Middle Ages to be a common appellation of Satan. (159)

From this misuse of the word *lucifer* arises then the misreading of the scripture passage on the part of the early Christian interpreters, a legacy of misreading inherited by readers who were to follow as each interpreted and continues to interpret a naming that is also a misnaming, a use of a word that is also a misuse of that word. From this misnaming, this misuse, this misreading, arise the differing chain of additional misreadings each time *lucifer* is the appellative substitute for Satan, the rebel upstart who sought to dethrone God.[21]

The "Luzbel" appearing in the early epigraphic poems of the first section of *Insistencias en Luzbel* is one more substitution in the chain of differing and deferring substitutions that have come to be associated with this name. In equating "Luzbel-Lucifer" with the fallen angel "Satan," and all that is associated with this latter appellation and the accompanying myth, the etymology of the Latin *lucifer* together with its subsequent (mis)use in both scripture and literary works has been "forgotten." In looking at Brines's epigraphic poem entitled "Luzbel," we see, then, that supposedly exact, equivalent namings in Brines's epigraph have led, instead, to inexact, unequivalent namings not only because the name "Luzbel" already has dismantled itself but also because language is duplicitious and thus, as Derrida has shown, "bears within itself the necessity of its own critique" (*SSP* 254).

In the differing chain of substitutions of *Insistencias en Luzbel*, the three epigraphic "Variations" found in the first part of the collection continue the acts of replacement and displacement already at work in the (mis)naming "Luzbel." In "Variación I" (Variation I) (*ED* 205) we find:

> (combate)
> Luchan Luzbel y el Angel.
> Todos somos la espada
> de Luzbel.

> (combat)
> Lucifer and the Angel struggle.
> We all are the sword
> of Lucifer.

Not linked essentially to a single referent, the name "Luzbel" recalls its own etymological root, the Latin *lux*, and thus the metaphoric and symbolic effects of the "light" of knowledge, wisdom, illumination. Here, however, such illumination is forever obscured by language struggling against itself whenever we (mis)read and (mis)use the naming "Luzbel." Sign is further replaced and displaced by sign when the differing figure of "el Angel" is developed in "Varación II" (Variation II) (*ED* 209):

> (desarrollo)
> El Angel no es Luzbel,
> mas Luzbel sí es el Angel:
> lo corrumpió el engaño.

> (development)
> The Angel is not Lucifer,
> but Lucifer is indeed the Angel:
> deceit corrupted him.

Combative language leads to repeated contradictions in terms where words, as "Esplendor negro" exhibits, "son tan sólo expresión de un engaño" (are only the expression of deceit) (line 15, *ED* 203) whenever the writer thinks she/he expresses what she/he thinks, whenever thought is contaminated, corrupted by deceptive naming. The writer, as the "Variación final" (Final variation) (*ED* 212) tells us, forever is concerned with the indeterminate nature of language:

> El Angel nada oculta:
> transparece.
> Luzbel oculta el rostro
> del que nada escribió:
> se vacío el ruido.

> The Angel conceals nothing:
> it is transparent.
> Lucifer conceals the face
> of the one who wrote nothing:
> the noise became empty.

Writing, as the varying "Insistences on Lucifer" show us, forever displays the writer's multiple attempts to name that which obstinately refuses an exact designation.[22]

What, then, do the "insistences" of *Insistencias en Luzbel* concern? The critic could turn to the epigraphs for written indications and descriptions summarizing the "main idea" of *Insistencias en Luzbel* and naming the collection's "central theme" in its various "inscriptions," recalling the Greek *epigraphein*. However, these epigraphs, as we have seen, repeatedly function against their own assertions as each inscribes "a systematic other message" behind or through what is being said" (Johnson, "Introduction" xiii). These inscriptions always already lead to differing "main ideas" and deferring namings of other "main ideas." Perhaps, then, the critic might opt for another strategy, that of providing a first reading of various poems of the collection where the poem under scrutiny is viewed as an emphatic, urgent statement regarding human being's efforts in coming to know the nature of "la nada." In such a reading the critic could view the poems of *Insistencias en Luzbel* as emphatic statements or persistent affirmations concerning the various reactions human being might have when pondering "la nada." It could then be argued that these urgent statements on both the nature of non-being and human being's response to this ontological possibility structure poems such as the following: "Esplendor negro" (Black splendor) (*ED* 203), "Desde el error" (From the error) (*ED* 209), "Entendimiento de una experiencia" (Understanding an experience) (*ED* 210 –211), "Tentaciones al acabar la tarde" (Temptations as the afternoon ends) (*ED* 221), "Otra vez Fausto" (Once again Faust) (*ED* 223), "Exabrupto" (Suddenly) (*ED* 230), "La realidad no permanece" (Reality does not last) (*ED* 233), and "No pido la inmortalidad" (I do not ask for immortality) (*ED* 238), among others.

Another critical approach to the repeated "insistences" of *Insistencias en Luzbel* might be pursued. The critic could trace these persistent demands to the speaker-writer's own inquiry into and attempts at comprehending the inadequacies of the medium employed: "las palabras son tan sólo expresión de un engaño" (words are only the expression of deceit) ("Esplendor negro") (*ED* 203). Persin, for example, argues that the speakers of "Esplendor negro" and "Actos de supresión" (Acts of suppression) (*ED* 208–9) "must face the perplexing conclusion that language is inadequate" (*RSP* 52–53). Or, an attempt could be made to reduce the multiple "insistences" to a common denominator, thereby naming the unifying concerns voiced in the repeated, urgent affirmations found throughout *Insistencias en Luzbel*. Some have urged, for example, that these "insistences" pertain to "the myth of existence" (Bradford, Debicki, Nantell, Persin). Others reduce these "insistences" to summarizing designations such as "the dialectic of nothingness" (Bradford); "la vida, vista a la luz de una eternidad problemática, y sin esperanza de recuperarse ni de tener efecto permanente, deja de tener sentido" (life, understood as a problematic eternity, and without hope for recovering nor of having a permanent effect, stops making sense) (Benson, "Convenciones" 8); "la experiencia de la nada . . . la experiencia de la vida" (the experience of nothingness . . . the experience of life) (Amusco, "Estética," 1); "una desolada metafísica de vaciedad y ruina . . . muerte, engaño y olvido" (a desolate metaphysics of emptiness and ruin . . . death, deceit and forgetfulness) (Villena, "Sobre *IEL*" 218); "insistir en La Nada . . . insistir en la vida" (to insist on Nothingness . . . to insist on life) (Jiménez, "Esplendor y apagamiento" 16); "el carácter unitario que el fracaso vital y el poético presentan para Brines" (the unitary character that vital and poetic ruin offer Brines (García Martín 199); and "La anticipación de la muerte y el vacío . . . la culpabilidad . . . el canto a la belleza del cuerpo humano, la exaltación del acto sexual" (The anticipation of death and the void . . . guilt . . . the song to the beauty of the human body, the exhaltation of the sexual act) (Sanz Echevarría 35, 42, 44). Although such critical strategies and approaches might be attempts at coming to name, and thereby hopefully know, the essence of the various "insistences" of *Insistencias en Luzbel*, the redoubling and repetition of differing "insistences" *about* the collection point to the redoubling and repetition of differing "insistences" *within* the collection, "insistences" that chart unceasingly the movement of *différance*.

The reader and the critic begin reading the numerous, insistent demands, declarations, assertions with the title of the collection, *Insistencias en Luzbel*, and this title involves not merely "insistences" but also "Luzbel." The figurative "Luzbel," as we have seen, is duplicitous, forever linked to a naming that is a misnaming. Any "Insistences on Lucifer" thus, will be problematic and will engender unsettling implications. Etymological retracing of the Spanish *insistir* (*DLE* 750) leads to the Latin *insistere*, "to set foot on, tread on, place oneself on" (*Cassell's Latin Dictionary* 314), which further leads to the root *sistere*, "to cause to stand, set, place; to make firm, settle firmly, establish" (*Cassell's Latin Dictionary* 558). The Spanish noun *insistencia* thus designates that action of "insisting," that action of "standing" on or upon a statement. The statement, however, the so-called "ground" upon which the poetic speakers' various "insistences" rest is the groundless ground named in the title, the groundless ground of the figurative, deceptive "Luzbel." The critic does not tread on a solid base, despite the title of the collection and despite the repeated "insistences" of many other critics. There is no secure footing in intertextual Christian lore since, as we have seen, a misreading of a specific scripture passage has led not only to the misnaming of Lucifer but also to the subsequent misinterpretations associated with this misnaming. The critic, thus, does not stand firmly upon the poet's own act of naming, designating, identifying. Rather, she/he finds her/himself on the weakened foundation of the act of naming itself where the movement of *différance* continually undermines both mastery of and confidence in naming.

As we have seen, attempts at describing, naming, defining the notion of "la nada" are common in Brines's poetry. At times, "la nada" goes by the name "la muerte" (death), as the speaker of "La mano no nos justifica" (The hand does not justify us), from *El otoño de las rosas* (*OR* 70), observes: "es la vida / espejo en que la muerte se contempla, / y en una sola inexistencia acaban" (life is / a mirror in which death contemplates itself, / and in only one nonexistence they end) (lines 27–29). Viewed differently by the poetic voice heard in "El encuentro" (The meeting) (*OR* 106), from this same collection, "La nada era el espejo en que me miré" (Nothingness is the mirror in which I looked at myself) (line 3). The poems "Esplendor negro" (Black splendor) (*ED* 203), "Entendimiento de una experiencia" (Understanding an experience) (*ED* 210–11), and "Identificación en un espejo" (Identification in a mirror) (*ED* 211–12), from *Insistencias en Luzbel,* all could be considered as additional attempts at describing the imagined experience of the terminus of human existence.[23] This experience is expressed and re-expressed in additional namings and renamings in various poems of *El otoño de las rosas.* The speaker of "Petición de mayor certeza" (Petition of great certainty) (*OR* 100) affirms, for example, in the poem's opening lines:

> Frente a todas las noches que vinieron
> y las escasas que me quedan,
> llegue la Noche yerta,
> la bolsa hueca y vana,
> en donde suena nada.   (lines 1–5)

> Facing all the nights that came
> and the few remaining for me,
> the motionless Night may arrive,
> the hollow and empty pouch,
> where nothing sounds.

The speaker of the brief poem entitled "Física de la muerte" (Physical death) (*OR* 102) presents the concept of "la nada" in this way:

> Prietas y extensas sombras nos acogen
> allí en las Humedades, fría Nada,
> después que nos fulmina el rayo blanco del Dios que no sabemos.

> Dense and extensive shadows shelter us
> there in the Dampness, chill Nothingness,
> After we have been wiped out by the white lightning of the God
> [we know nothing about.

In "Tríptico de la aventura" (Triptych of the adventure) (*OR* 97), a poem reminiscent in both theme and style of *Insistencias en Luzbel*, we find yet another attempt at describing both the "myth" and the "destiny" of human existence:

> (*mito*)
> Cierta vez fue la vida
> un mágico transcurso,
> un tránsito sin fin.

> (*realidad*)
> Lo que perdí, y lo que ya no espero,
> aunque exista quizás.   5
> Y este presente atónito de ser.

> (*destino*)
> Esta espera del tiempo aún,
> el calor y la rosa.
> Después la ceguedad de ese dios Hueco.

> (*myth*)
> At a certain time life was
> a magical course of time,
> a passage without end.

> (*reality*)
> What I lost, and what I now no longer hope,
> although it may perhaps exist.   5
> And this astonished present moment of being.

> (*destiny*)
> This waiting for time as yet,
> the passion and the rose.
> Afterwards the blindness of that Hollow god.

In other poems of *El otoño de las rosas*, however, the reader is presented with texts concerning not the fictionalized imaginings of what "la nada" might be but rather the personal experience of what being incessantly becomes *within* each present instant of human being's existence. Put differently, in poems such as "Días de invierno en la casa de verano" (Winter days in the summer house) (*OR* 15–17), "Ante el jardín nublado" (In the presence of the cloudy garden) (*OR* 39–40), "Con un ramo de rosas" (With a bouquet of roses) (*OR* 74), "El más hermoso territorio" (The most beautiful territory) (*OR* 92–94), "Las últimas preguntas" (The final questions) (*OR* 108–109), "El ojo solitario de la noche" (The solitary eye of night) (*OR* 111), and "El oscuro oye cantar la luz" (Darkness listens to light singing) (*OR* 112–13), to name only a few, the speakers, while living *within* the present instant, repeatedly witness "el sonido apagado de la vida" (the extinguished sound of life) (line 12, "Días de invierno en la casa de verano" [Winter days in the summer house] *OR* 15). As each of these speakers undergo and scrutinize the personal act of existing *within* the present moment each also encounters and endures personal being ceaselessly becoming non-being. The speaker of "Ante el jardín nublado" (In the presence of the cloudy garden) (*OR* 39–40) describes this existential mode with and by means of the question "¿ . . . y a dónde va mi vida / que ya no está?" (and where is my life going / now that it is not?) (lines 7–8). The speaker-writer of "El ojo solitario de la noche" (The solitary eye of night) (*OR* 111) characterizes ephemeral existence in this way: "Escribo estas palabras, y no entiendo / por qué tan sólo soy (y que no soy) / la confusión de unos sordos sonidos" (I write these words, and I do not understand / why I only am (and that I am not) / the confusion of some stifled sounds) (lines 17–19).

"Las últimas preguntas" (The final questions) (*OR* 108–9) presents the reader with the constant oscillation of being and nonbeing *within* the present temporal moment of human being's existence, an event the poetic voice openly interrogates. In this illustrative poem, the speaker's personal experience of being "sin tiempo" (without time) (line 14), suspended *within* the present moment that is ceaselessly becoming past, leads this poetic voice to question repeatedly the present existential condition of (non)being:

En el acabamiento de la tarde,
cuando hacía el camino, he llegado de pronto
       ¿a dónde?

La noche que ha caído, tan repentina y negra, me impide ver,
y sólo sé que nadie me acompaña.   5
¿Qué ha sido este viaje?
      Muy largo debió ser, por la fatiga,
o acaso fue muy breve, si existió:
no puedo recobrar el olor de las rosas.
De entre mis posesiones   10
sólo guardo un pañuelo que oscurece en mis manos:
¿para secar las lágrimas que no puedo verter?
¿o para despedirme, desde la Prescripción, de las sombras que dejo?

Sin tiempo, me pregunto: ¿qué soy? ¿quién soy? ¿y para qué partí?
¿Y qué sentido tiene haber llegado?   15

Y qué poco me importa lo que, del lado del desuso, pueda pasar
                                                                [ahora,
si nada entiendo.
Dejo de ser mortal. Mas no soy inmortal.
Como si nada hubiera sido.

In the completion of the afternoon,
when I was making my way, I arrived suddenly
                                        where?

Night has fallen, so suddenly and black, it prevents me from seeing,
and I only know that no one accompanies me.   5
What has this trip been?
              It should have been very long, due to the fatigue,
or perhaps it was very brief, if it existed:
I cannot recover the fragrance of the roses.
Among my possessions   10
I only keep a handkerchief that grows dark in my hands:
to dry the tears that I cannot shed?
or to say goodbye, from the Prescription, to the shadows I leave?

Without time, I ask myself: What am I? Who am I? And for what
                                        [reason did I depart?
And what is the meaning of having arrived?   15
And how little what, on the verge of disuse, may happen
                                        [now matters to me,
if I understand nothing.
I stop being mortal. But I am not immortal.
As if nothing had been.

As in other poems from Brines's collections, the fading afternoon
(line 1) and the arrival of nightfall (line 4) are metaphoric constructs
aiding the first-person speaker's meditative exploration of ultimate
personal finitude (lines 6 –9). A first reading of the poem could establish that the symbolic "viaje" (trip) of lines 6 –15 is that of life, a common, even clichéd, literary motif. In the poem, the poetic voice experiences and questions both the occurrence (lines 6 –9) and the purpose
of this existential journey (lines 13–15). This reading could be sustained by line 17, "si nada entiendo" (if I understand nothing), when the
speaker finally reaches and thereby comes to know the ultimate desti-
nation of the journey of human existence. The poem's title, in this reading, would then point to the series of "final questions" asked by human
being (lines 6, 14, 15) as he/she seeks to comprehend "la nada" (line
17) while living out personal existence.
    The poetic speaker's act of questioning could be a stance the critic

might adopt. The noun *preguntas*, of the title of the poem, leads her/him directly to the notion of questioning. The poem's title points to an inquiry that is about to take place and/or has taken place and/or will take place and this inquiry, it seems, involves plural *preguntas*. The repeated yet varying questionings of lines 3, 6, 12, 13, 14, and 15 not only form the structural basis of the poetic text but also further the critical, redoubled interrogation as the critic begins to relate and interrelate these questions, inquire into the questions themselves, and even furnish possible answers. The derivational source for the verb *preguntar* is the Latin verb *percontari*, and as Corominas points out: "se trata de un derivado de *contus* 'bichero, percha', con el sentido primitivo de 'buscar el fondo del mar o río,' 'sondear,' y de ahí 'someter a un interrogatorio'" (it concerns a derivative of *contus* 'boat-hook, pole,' with the primitive sense of 'searching the bottom of the sea or river,' 'to fathom,' and from there 'to subject to an interrogation' (*DCE*, Vol. 4, 635). The critical exploratory act of "fathoming" the poem thus further probes and even extends the interrogation already begun by the poetic text.

If the critic begins such a critical inquiry with the poem's title it seems, at first, that she/he is about to encounter "final," "last" questions that signal, as the Latin *ultimare* indicates, that the questioning has come to or is about "to come to an end" (*H* 1925). Perhaps these questions are the "last" queries in a series of queries begun earlier in *El otoño de las rosas*, or earlier in the poetry of the collections written before 1986. After all, the poem's first-person voice speaks "desde la Prescripción" (from the Prescription) (line 13). A retracing of the Latin root *praescribere*, to write before, to set before in writing (*DLE* 1061; *Cassell's Latin Dictionary* 467), could lead to this conclusion. If these questions, however, are "últimas preguntas" are they really as "final" as the text might lead the critic to believe in an initial reading of the poem? Ultimately, the critic might explore the text searching for the "final" question among the series of final questions provided. However, which of these questions is the "last" query? The one that happens to come last in the series (line 15)? Or, are there yet other questions, as the title seems to suggest, which are situated the farthest beyond and thus are the most distant, the most remote, recalling the Latin *ulter* and its superlative form *ultimus* (*H* 1925), of this series?

The naming of "Las últimas preguntas" (The final questions) occurs at the beginning of the poem in the poem's title, and also within the poem's text, and also in what seems to be the last question of the many questions asked (line 15). Are these questions as "terminal" as we are told they are if more questions continue to be asked? If such questions are "últimas preguntas" why do they continue within and eventually infiltrate, even subvert, many of the assertions of the text? For example, in lines 7, 8 and 9 the speaker attempts to furnish an answer to the question asked in line 6:

> ¿Qué ha sido este viaje?
>   Muy largo debió ser, por la fatiga,
> o acaso fue muy breve, si existió:
> no puedo recobrar el olor de las rosas.   (lines 6–9)

> What has this trip been?
>   It should have been very long, due to the fatigue
> or perhaps it was very brief, if it existed:
> I cannot recover the fragrance of the roses.

Such contradictory declarations lead the critic to question how such a "viaje" could be both "long" and "short" and also if such a "trip" even took place at all. In line 18, the critic encounters two declarative sentences which assert, paradoxically, the speaker's simultaneous state of being neither mortal nor immortal: "Dejo de ser mortal. Mas no soy inmortal" (I stop being mortal. But I am not immortal). When the poem ends with this contradiction does not the critic encounter an additional embedded question, even questions? If the poem's speaker is no longer mortal and also is not immortal then what *is* this *yo*? What *is* the speaker's state or mode of being? Moreover, if the questions asked in the poem are "últimas preguntas," as the title implies, do we not also have other questions that underlie the final hypothetical, dangling statement: "Como si nada hubiera sido" (As if nothing had been) (line 19)? What exactly is this "nada?" And why is its state or condition contrary to past fact? What is the past fact that is indirectly alluded to yet not directly explained? If the questions asked in the poem's text are the "last," "final," "terminal" questions, why do they stubbornly continue in the speaker's assertions? In "Las últimas preguntas," the critic does not encounter answers to the "últimas preguntas" but rather a chain of differing and deferring substitutions of questions for more questions that are repeatedly doubled and redoubled throughout both the poetic inquiry and the critic's critical questioning of that inquiry.

The Spanish verb *preguntar*, to question, ask, inquire, demand, from which the noun *pregunta* is formed, as we have seen, has at its root the Latin *percontari*, "to sound with a pole; hence, to inquire, interrogate, question, investigate" (*Cassell's Latin Dictionary* 1335). Earnest examination of what appears to be a singular root, however, leads to differing and deferred semantic retracings for the Spanish *preguntar*, a verb that also has another etymological origin, that of the vulgar Latin *per-*

cunctari. As Corominas notes, the Latin *cunctari* denotes "dudar, vac-ilar" (to doubt, to vacilate) (*DCE*, Vol. 4, 635). A determinate "mean-ing" of the Spanish noun *pregunta*, thus, cannot be traced to a single root that will explain it concisely since this term is itself unwilling to be reduced to a single etymological source, a definitive explication.[24] The term *pregunta* entails, then, both the notions of inquiry and doubt, inquiry originating in doubt *and* doubt resulting from inquiry. The speaker's and the critic's search for any possible underlying unity, any essential and fixed "meaning" in both the naming "últimas preguntas" and in the asking of "últimas preguntas" is shadowed by the question-ing of underlying, deceptive differences already at work in the spuri-ous term *pregunta*.

"Las últimas preguntas" is not a self-enclosed literary text furnish-ing "final" questions and "final" answers, as the title might lead us to believe. The critic's act of interrogating this text and commenting on this interrogation extends the poetic text, furthers it along, opens it up even more to the dialogue of questions already begun by the act of inquiry initiated in the poem. The "últimas preguntas" suggested by the poem's title are not the "last" in a series. On the contrary, each repeatedly vacillates with the inception of still another, and still yet another question asked by the poem's speaker, by the critic, and by additional critical commentators who will, in turn, supply, supplement, add to, replace, and displace the queries begun but never finished by the poetic text and the critic's interrogation of that poetic text.

Many of the questions asked within this poetic speaker's dialogue of questions arise from the experience of (non)being *within* the present, temporal instant, an instant repeatedly highlighted in "Las últimas pre-guntas" (lines 4, 5, 11, 12, 13, 14, 15, 16, 17, 18). In one such series of queries the speaker asks: "Sin tiempo, me pregunto: ¿qué soy? ¿quién soy? ¿y para qué partí? / ¿Y qué sentido tiene haber llegado?" (With-out time, I ask myself: What am I? Who am I? And for what reason did I depart? / And what is the meaning of having arrived?) (lines 14–15). Returning briefly to the journey motif developed earlier in the text and in the first reading of the poem, the speaker seems to be ques-tioning the purpose of undertaking the metaphoric "trip" along the road of human existence. Another differing, albeit antiquated, "meaning" of the Spanish verb *partir*, however, takes into account the act of final-izing, concluding or finishing something (*DLE* 983). Thus, at one and the same time, the speaker seems both to be about to begin the journey of existence and in the midst of finalizing this same existential "trip." The Spanish verb *partir*, from the Latin *partire* (*DLE* 983), denotes fur-ther the act of dividing or separating something into two or more parts. Has the speaker's personal existence been divided? If so, what constitutes this division: "¿qué soy? ¿quién soy?" (What am I? Who am I?) (line 14)? Or, has the speaker witnessed repeatedly, with each ephemeral, present moment, what seems to be the relentless separation of being from nonbeing as human being incessantly becomes that which he/she is(not)? This existential "division" is hardly definitive, final, determinate, however, because each time the speaker questions the possible "division" of being from nonbeing the speaker also puts into question the "division" itself since the interrogation of each existential mode itself reveals that each no longer is opposed to nor divided from the other, but rather each is its own difference from itself *within* the present instant.[25]

The speaker lives *and* lives out personal existence *within* each present moment (lines 6 – 9; 12–13; 14 –17) and writes about this contradictory existential mode "desde la Prescripción" (line 13): from the perspective of what he has written and described before. The term *prescripción*, however, tracing a now antiquated use of the word, also denotes a limitation, a restriction, a restraint (*DLE* 1061). Perhaps the speaker, now writer, writes "desde la Prescripción" because writing always takes place within or from the limitation of being. The speaker's metaphoric "journey" of life, in a sense, has been limited from its very beginning: "Mas no soy inmortal" (But I am not immortal) (line 18). Is not human mortality, then, the final limitation from which this speaker-writer might write about human existence? This speaker, however, is not concerned with the ephemeral nature of his entire lifetime, as the first reading suggests, as much as the speaker is concerned with (non)being *within* the present instant and writing about and interrogating this paradoxical existential mode *within* the present instant (lines 10 –13).

In the poem "El encuentro" (The meeting), from *El otoño de las rosas* (107), the first-person speaker describes in yet another way "la nada."

> Al fin nos presentaron: Aquí la nada. Este, es el que es.
> Yo me acerqué. Alguien tendió la mano. Yo la esquivé.
> La nada era el espejo en el que me miré.

> At last they introduced us: That one is nothingness. This one, is the
> [one who exists.
> I approached. Someone extended a hand. I avoided it.
> Nothingness was the mirror in which I looked at myself.

A first reading of the poem could argue that the speaker is describing the imagined experience of "meeting" the now personified "la nada" at the end of the speaker's life: "Al fin nos presentaron" (At last they introduced us) (line 1). The repeated preterite actions describing what took place during this "encounter"—"me acerqué" (I approached), "tendió" (stretched out), "esquivé" (avoided), "me miré" (I looked at myself) further sustain the depiction of "la nada" as the terminus. This "meeting," however, is both welcome ("Yo me acerqué. Alguien tendió la mano" [I approached. Someone extended a hand]) and unwelcome ("Y la esquivé" [I avoided it]) as the *yo* both participates in this "meeting" and yet seeks to keep clear of direct contact with the personified "la nada." Such evasion, however, is impossible whenever human being fully contemplates and is directly conscious of the ultimate finitude of personal being: "La nada era el espejo en que me miré" (Nothingness was the mirror in which I looked at myself).

This first-person speaker, however, does not "meet" with "la nada" at the end of his lifetime, as the first reading suggests and as the poem's opening line might lead the critic to believe. Rather, this "meeting" repeatedly takes place and already has taken place while the speaker is engaged in the act of being. We are not focusing on the end of a human being's lifetime but rather on the act of existing *within* the continuous series of terminal present moments that are continually becoming past. The "encounter" named and renamed, presented and represented in this poem is that of humankind's ceaseless experience of spurious being. The shadow presence of the absence of being always accompanies being, meets with being, encounters being, oscillates with being whenever human being lives out each present moment.

The naming and renaming of the experience of this "encounter" in this poem take the critic to the opposition, the confrontation between what seem, at first, to be two adversarial modes of being, especially if she/he recalls the root of the Spanish noun *encuentro*, the Latin *contra*, "opposite, in opposition to, against, contrary to, opposed to" (*H* 452). This "opposition" could be summarized in the hierarchical organization and naming of the duality as being/nonbeing. One existential state thus "meets" the other existential state as adversary would meet adversary in what might be called a face to face confrontation between two antithetical, ontological modes. However, is there really an existential battle taking place? Or rather, are we not witnessing the skirmish occurring within signification whenever the supplement comes into play? When the identity of each of these existential modes is put into question, rather than viewed as adversarial, then the focus shifts from the conflictual structure of the opposition to the "phase of overturning," the "interval between inversion" (*POS* 41; 42) when the mode of (non)being emerges *within* each moment and thus marks the repeated experience of "La nada era el espejo en el que me miré" (Nothingness was the mirror in which I looked at myself).

Over the last thirty years Francisco Brines's poetry names and re-names "la nada." These repeated attempts could lead the critic to believe that this poetry is a poetry in search of a foundation on which the ultimate, absolute, determinate "definition of nothingness" will be based and upon which this definition, finally, will rest. Insistent definitions and redefinitions throughout Brines's poetry lead the critic easily to such a conclusion. Such definitions and redefinitions could be viewed, thus, as multiple examples and indications of the poet's repeated attempts at getting this concept right, of naming this concept once and for all in a singular, unequivocal, determinate naming. The poet's quest, then, could serve as the catalyst for the critic's own quest of tracing and retracing the naming of "la nada" in Brines's poetry whenever she/he attempts to reduce these different namings to a singular naming by means of the act of interpretation.

We have seen, however, that both the poet's and the critic's activity of naming and renaming leads not to an exclusive naming but rather to a multiplicity of differing denominations. In Brines's poetry, the concept of "la nada" is not reduced to a singular essence that is always the same, a singular essence designated and defined always in the same way, always by the same name. Rather, this ontological mode is extended by the "conflictuality of *différance*" (*POS* 44) evident in naming. The multiple attempts at designating "la nada," on the part of the poet, and at interpreting and interrogating these many namings, on the part of the critic, point to both the excess *and* the inadequation apparent in naming.

Afterword

> ... deconstruction is an attitude that examines the force of
> power and authority in the text as a desire for mastery—the
> attempt to master knowledge through language, and meaning
> through interpretation—a desire that textuality ultimately
> subverts, for writing always already has begun to deconstruct
> itself.   —Danny Anderson

Francisco Brines's poetry clearly demonstrates a postmodern aesthetics in its constant questioning of the duplicitous nature of language. As the preceding chapters make evident, Brines's interrogation of three of the fundamental concerns of human being, concerns phrased in the form of the questions "What is knowledge?" "What is time?," and "What is nonbeing?" leads him to explore in his poetry not only possible responses to these queries but also the role language plays in formulating these responses. Brines's dual activity of questioning and answering takes him to one final concern highlighted throughout my study: language engaged in a relentless, semantic stuggle with itself forever complicates and obfuscates the poet's replies.

Deconstruction repeatedly reminds us of the battleground of signification and thus is a particularly useful mode of analysis for Brines's poetry. The critic willing to activate and participate in the deconstructive enterprise[1] learns that the interpretive act, like the poetic act, is subject to the duplicitous nature of the medium employed. It should be apparent from the preceding chapters that the critic's language about the poet's language does not elucidate the poem's ultimate "meaning," if one such "meaning" even could be elucidated, but rather it complicates it even more by focusing on the semantic perplexities at work and at play *within* the very language utilized. The deconstructive attitude provides the critic, as we have seen throughout this study, with a way to engage in questioning language and its slippery and deceptive nature. Deconstruction, thus, continually reminds us that language is *différance*.

The deconstructive critical readings of many of Brines's poems examined in my study have shown that language, both the poet's and the critic's, unceasingly is at war with itself whenever sign clashes with sign, sign undermines sign, sign substitutes for sign, sign is allowed to be and become what it most playfully is: a "structure of difference," as Spivak underscores (xvii). Both the ground of language and the search for ground, in both the poetic and the critical texts, always already are ungrounded whenever textuality subverts determinate signification. My readings of Brines's poetry point out the deconstructive and disseminative effects of language used to question the act of naming and the act of knowing through and by means of naming. In these various readings, poet, poetic speaker, and critic repeatedly find themselves in the grasp of knowledge shadowed by ignorance, in the midst of the present moment unceasingly becoming past, in the entanglement that is the act of naming by means of differing *and* deferring substitutions. My readings demonstrate that the critic cannot break out of the endless chain of supplementary differences (under)mining the act of naming, nor is the critic able to escape from the temporality of her/his own endeavor, nor does the critic, ultimately, master knowledge through language. Did not the numerous speakers of Brines's poems examined in this work discover (in blindness? with insight?) that these differences, in a very real way, endlessly both constitute *and* dismantle human existence? The critical readings offered here, finally, forever point to the deconstructability of both human existence and writing about human existence. My interrogation of Francisco Brines's poetry, like the poetry itself, scrutinizes the innumerable, diverse, and often conflicting aspects of language repeatedly engaged in a semantic struggle with itself.

Notes

Introduction

1. Brines's poetic works include *Las brasas* (The embers); *El Santo inocente* (The innocent saint); *Palabras a la oscuridad* (Words to darkness); *Aún no* (Not yet). These were subsequently published in the 1974 collection *Poesía 1960–1970: Ensayo de una despedida* (Poetry 1960–1970: A farewell essay), where *El Santo inocente* appeared with the new title *Materia narrativa inexacta* (Inexact narrative matter). In 1977 Brines published *Insistencias en Luzbel* (Insistences on Lucifer). The aforementioned works were later published in the 1984 collection *Poesía 1960–1977: Ensayo de una despedida;* the cover erroneously lists the dates 1960–81. Also in 1984 Brines published *Selección propia* (My own selection), which includes his most extensive commentary on his poetry to date, "La certidumbre de la poesía" (The certitude of poetry). Since 1985, Brines has published the following collections: *Poemas excluidos* (Excluded poems) (1985); *Poemas a D.K.* (Poems to D. K.) (1986); and *El otoño de las rosas* (The autumn of the roses) (1986).

It is very fitting that Brines's collection and recollection of his poems in a single volume, first in 1974 and later in 1984, are entitled *Ensayo de una despedida* (A farewell essay). In "La certidumbre de la poesía" Brines comments:

> Cuando tuve que reunir mis libros en un volumen, el conjunto lo titulé *Ensayo de una despedida*, buscando en él su significación esencial. Se trata, por un lado, de la despedida de la vida, concepto que se nos hace presente cuando, ya muy pronto, tomamos conciencia de nuestro destino mortal. Por otro, esta despedida es también la conciencia de las sucesivas pérdidas en que consiste el vivir. Asistimos a un empobrecimiento sin pausa desde la adolescencia a la vejez. Empezamos por perder la inmortalidad y, después, la inocencia. Es decir, dejamos de ser dioses y nos convertimos en culpables. (SP 20)

> When I had to collect my books of poetry in one volume, I entitled the grouping A farewell essay, searching there for its essential meaning. It concerns, on one hand, the goodbye from life, the concept that becomes apparent to us, very early on, when we become conscious of our mortal destiny. On the other hand, this goodbye is also the awareness of the successive losses that constitute living. We witness a relentless impoverishment from adolescence to old age. We begin by losing immortality and, later, innocence. That is to say, we stop being gods and we become culpable beings.

A number of critics have studied Brines's poetry. Bousoño's "Situación y características de la poesía de Francisco Brines," Debicki's "Francisco Brines: Text and Reader" (*PD* 20–39), Jiménez's "La poesía de Francisco Brines (Sobre *Las brasas*)" (Jiménez, *Cinco poetas* 417–75) and "Realidad y misterio en *Palabras a la oscuridad* de Francisco Brines" (*Diez años* 175–204), and Persin's "Francisco Brines: Toward the Limits of Language and Being" (*RSP* 45–67) are fundamental critical studies. In addition, I shall mention here those critical works that have most influenced my readings and rereadings of Brines's poetry: Aldrich; Amusco ("Algunos aspectos" and "Estética de la nada"); Benson ("Convenciones de lenguaje" and "Memory, Tradition and the Reader"); Bradford ("The Dialectic of Nothingness" and "Two Recent Approaches"); Cañas ("Introducción" to *El rumor del tiempo* and *Poesía y percepción);* Jiménez ("Esplendor y apagamiento"); Sanz Echevarría ("La insistencia de Francisco Brines"); Simón ("Algunos aspectos en la sátira de Francisco Brines"); and Villena ("Sobre *Insistencias en Luzbel"*). Finally, my own articles on the poetry of Francisco Brines have contributed to my evolving views on not only his poetic texts but also the interimplication of theory and practice.

2. Although the Spanish noun *hombre* would normally be rendered into English as "man," "mankind," I have opted to use a less gender-specific term. I do this whenever possible in both my translations and my critical commentary, utilizing, for example, the more all-encompassing term "humankind." Some of Brines's poems, however, feature a male poetic voice. In other poems the gender of the speaker is ambiguous. For the sake of consistency, I have adopted the stylistic convention of assuming the presence of a male poetic voice in Brines's poetry and in my translations of his poetry, since the poet is male, although I recognize and emphasize in my study that this poetry addresses existential concerns pertaining to us all.

3. Suffice it to say that the works of Debicki (*PD*) and Persin (*RSP*) are important contributions on the critical literature of the "Generation of 1956–71." In addition, the works of Badosa; Bousoño (*Poesía poscontemporánea*); Cano; García Martín; and Jiménez (*Diez años*) should not be overlooked. Other studies influential to my approaches to this group of poets include: Alvarado Tenorio; Batlló; Díaz; García de la Concha (*La poesía española de la posguerra*); García Hortelano; González Muela; Grande; Hernández; Jiménez ("Medio siglo" and "Poética y poesía"); Mantero; Marra-López ("Una nueva" and "La poesía"); Martínez Ruiz; Quiñones; Rubio ("La poesía española" and "Teoría y polémica"); Silver. Also see the special 1988 issue of *Insula* entitled *Encuentro con el 50*. Recently, a few significant studies concerning contemporary Spanish poetry have stressed the problems encountered when the critic attempts to categorize the poets and the poetry of contemporary Spain in generational groupings. Debicki, for example, urges the critical need for reappraising the poetry of contemporary Spain and viewing it from the perspective of "the emergence of a postmodern aesthetics, in this period" ("Critical Perspectives" 8). I heartily concur, and my study offers one such reappraisal. In addition, see Debicki, "Poesía española de la postmodernidad," "Una poesía," and "New Poets," and Jiménez's recent "Fifty Years of Contemporary Spanish Poetry (1939–1989)," where he questions the generational scheme and examines, instead, literary periods in contemporary Spain.

4. Jonathan Culler explains, "The supplement is an inessential extra, added to something complete in itself, but the supplement is added in order to complete, to compensate for a lack in what was supposed to be complete in itself. These two different meanings of supplement are linked in a powerful logic, and in both meanings the supplement is presented as exterior, foreign to the 'essential' nature of that to which it is added or in which it is substituted" (103).

5. Derrida's clever and playful coining of the term *différance* is discussed in "Différance" (*DIF* 7–9, especially) and *Positions* (*POS* 39–40). Throughout my study, I refer

to English editions of cited Derridean texts whenever possible. Bibliographical information regarding the original work in French is provided in the Works Cited. Concerning the notion of *différance*, Jonathan Culler observes: "The verb *différer* means to differ and to defer. *Différance* sounds exactly the same as *différence*, but the ending *ance*, which is used to produce verbal nouns, makes it a new form meaning 'difference-differing-deferring.' *Différance* thus designates both a 'passive' difference already in place as the condition of signification and an act of differing which produces differences" (97).

6. Throughout my study, I use the term *human being* in the metaphysical sense of "human life."

7. Frequently in deconstructive theory and criticism the phrase *always already* is used not only to underscore contextual instability but also to emphasize the supplementary play of meaning. I employ this same phrase in my study when I wish to call attention to the play of difference.

Chapter 1. Questioning Epistemological Ground

1. See Debicki's introductory chapter (*PD*, especially pages 6–9), and Persin's opening chapter (*RSP*, particularly pages 15–22). Also see Cano (133–40), and Jiménez (*Diez años* 15–32) for excellent summaries of the vision of poetry espoused by the poets of this generation. In addition, see the anthologies of Batlló, Martínez-Ruiz, Molina, and Ribes.

2. According to Derrida, "It is because of *différance* that the movement of signification is possible only if each so-called 'present' element, each element appearing on the scene of presence, is related to something other than itself, thereby keeping within itself the mark of the past element, and already letting itself be vitiated by the mark of its relation to the future element, this trace being related no less to what is called the future than to what is called the past, and constituting what is called the present by means of this very relation to what it is not: what it absolutely is not, not even a past or a future as a modified present" (*DIF* 13). Spivak observes in the "Translator's Preface" to Derrida's *Of Grammatology*, "The structure of the sign is determined by the trace or track of that other which is forever absent" (xvii). Culler notes, "The arbitrary nature of the sign and the system with no positive terms give us the paradoxical notion of an 'instituted trace,' a structure of infinite referral in which there are only traces—traces prior to any entity of which they might be the trace" (99). For a discussion of the Derridian notion of the trace see Atkins (*RD* 18–27).

3. As Atkins explains, "the newly elevated term is reinscribed in the field of language and shown to oscillate ceaselessly with its apparent opposite. Thus to reverse the hierarchy only so as to displace the reversal; to unravel in order to reconstitute what is always already inscribed" (*RD* 84–85).

4. For a detailed consideration of *différance*, consult Derrida, "Différance," particularly pages 1–27. In the 1980's, Valente and Brines, among others of this group of poets, began to rethink their earlier *poéticas* and, consequently, their approaches to poetry as knowledge. Valente, for example, observes in a 1980 *El País* interview: "Yo vería hoy la poesía más bien como un inconocimiento" (Today I would see poetry rather as nonknowledge) (7). In "La certidumbre de la poesía" Brines affirms: "Creo que la evolución expresiva de mi poesía ha ido en dirección de ese encuentro conjunto de ambigüedad y lucidez" (I believe that the expressive evolution of my poetry has gone in the direction of that conjunct encounter of ambiguity and clarity) (*SP* 14–15). In "A manera de un comentario" (In the manner of a commentary) Rodríguez observes: "Si la poesía, entre

otras cosas, es una búsqueda, o una participación entre la realidad y la experiencia poética de ella a través del lenguaje, claro está que cada poema es como una especie de acoso
para lograr (meta imposible) dichos fines" (If poetry, among other things, is a search, or
a participation in reality and the poetic experience of reality by means of language, clearly every poem is a type of pursuit for obtaining [impossible goal] these ends) (*Desde mis
poemas* 13).

   5. All quotations from Rodríguez's poetry are from *Desde mis poemas.* Quotations
from Valente's poetry are from *Punto cero.* All citations are followed by line numbers
and page numbers, when appropriate.

   6. In Spanish, the noun *jornal*, from the Latin *diurnus*, "of or belonging to the day"
(*H* 600), denotes day-work, day-wages, and journey-work, and thus conveys both the
daily work and the daily stipend. Critical studies of Rodríguez's poetry abound. Jonathan
Mayhew's recent *Claudio Rodríguez and the Language of Poetic Vision*, Debicki's
"Claudio Rodríguez: Language Codes and Their Effects" (*PD* 40–58) and Persin's "The
Syntax of Assertion in the Poetry of Claudio Rodríguez" (*RSP* 68–97) are fundamental
critical works. In addition, Bousoño's "La poesía de Claudio Rodríguez" is a cornerstone
critical study. I shall mention here those works that have most influenced my readings
of his poetry: Bradford ("Two Recent Approaches" and "Transcendent Reality");
Jiménez ("Claudio Rodríguez" and "Hacia la verdad"); M. L. Miller ("Elementos
metapóeticos" and "Linguistic Skepticism"); Mudrovic ("Progression of Distance,"
"Time and Reality," "Claudio Rodríguez's 'Alianza y condena,'" and "The Poetry of
Claudio Rodríguez"; Nuñez; Prieto de Paula; and Sala.

   7. Bradford examines Rodríguez's "search for illumination through concrete reality" ("Two Recent Approaches" 33) and uses "Alto jornal" as an example. She observes
that in this poem "the poet seeks illumination through everyday experiences in the world"
("Two Recent Approaches" 31). Bousoño investigates Rodríguez's *Conjuros* and his use
of a special type of metaphor, the "alegoría disémica," which points to the transcendental meaning of the poem. For Bousoño, the metaphor "alto jornal" is one such disemic
allegory ("La poesía de Claudio Rodríquez" 13–15). Mudrovic further notes, "In this
poem Rodríguez converts the routine departure for work into the discovery of a new out-
look on life" ("The Progression of Distance" 330).

   8. Etymological overtones of the Latin follow. *Communicare*: to communicate,
unite, share with another. *Communio*: communion, mutual participation, *Communitas*:
fellowship, society. These all underlie the Spanish verb *comulga* in Rodríguez's poem.
The *Etymological Dictionary of Latin* also notes that in such words as *communis, communitas, communio, communicare*, "Two senses (ult. from the same *mei-*) have coa-
lesced, viz. 'exchange' and 'bind.' For the latter v. *moenia, munia, municipium*; for the
former v. *muto, mutuus. Commumis* is thus = 'sharing in common' and also 'bound
together'" (62).

   9. The etymological senses of the verb *caber*, from the Latin *capere*, "to take in, to
take, to hold," at once stress the notion of having room or capacity for, containing one
thing within another, and taking in with the mind or senses (*DCE* 710; *DLE* 215).

   10. *Pellejo,* derived from the Latin *pellicula*, which is the diminutive form of *pellis*,
denotes at it root a small skin or hide (*H* 1325). In Spanish, it is usually used when refer-
ring to skin that has been removed from an animal.

   11. See Paul De Man's "Semiology and Rhetoric" for an excellent discussion of the
confrontation between the literal and the figural in Yeats's "Among School Children."
Persin observes of Rodríguez and his work: "This poet's techniques of assertion, like his
lexical experimentation, work on two different levels. The poet on the one hand purports
to describe, explain, clarify, and illuminate; but on the other, he forces the reader to consider alternative and contradictory possibilities of signification" ("Syntax of Assertion"

68–69). She further stresses that in Rodríguez's poetry, "The reader is thus confronted with texts whose contradictory interpretive paths of significance continually subvert one another" (93). M. L. Miller investigates "la índole problemática del lenguaje" (The problematic character of language) in Rodríguez's "Siempre la claridad viene del cielo" (Clarity always comes from the sky), focusing on the irreconcilable differences, contradictions, and ambiguities of this particular text ("Elementos metapoéticos" 131). In this poem, she highlights a series of elements that "pueden interpretarse de más de una manera y que incluso encierran significados contrarios y hasta incompatibles" (can be interpreted in more than one way including embracing contradictory and even incompatible meanings) (129), elements that repeatedly undermine "la claridad." Her observations could also be applicable to "Alto jornal."

12. Debicki's "José Angel Valente: Reading and Rereading" (*PD* 102–22) and Persin's "Theories of Language in José Angel Valente's *Poemas a Lázaro*" (*RSP* 26–44) examine Valente's "poética" and emphasize the creative act as a way of coming to know reality. Debicki's focus is on undertaking a second reading of specific poems by Valente, "a second reading . . . oriented at perceiving signs and linguistic codes which are not at first evident, but which nevertheless underlie its full significance. This significance is often not apparent at a poem's basic or representational level, but emerges when we pay attention to verbal patterns which redirect our reading and help us to see a new focus and unity" (*PD* 103). Persin's study, on the other hand, examines "Primer poema," among others from *Poemas a Lázaro*, showing that in this poetic text "Both poet and reader must approach the language of poetry as a starting point: poet, word, idea, and reader all participate in the ongoing process of the creative act" (*RSP* 27). Sherno also examines this poem and the poet's role in the search for knowledge and truth (166–68). Studies of Valente's poetry are numerous. Persin's significant, critical work should not go unnoticed. See, for example, "The Anxiety of Influence" (*RSP* 26–44), and "Poem as Process." Also, Anita Hart's sustained inquiry into Valente's poetry marks an important contribution. See, in particular, "Metapoetic Texts," "Poetry of Illumination, "Poetry and Language," and "The Poet, the Word and the Reader". Other important studies essential to my own approaches to Valente's poetic texts are listed here: Bousoño ("La poesia de José Angel Valente"); Cañas (*Poesía y percepción*); Daydí-Tolson; Debicki ("Intertextuality and Reader-Response"); Jiménez ("Lucha, duda, y fe"); Lertora; Marra-López ("La poesía"); Martino; Mas; Polo; Risco; and Ugalde.

13. Sherno comes to the following conclusion: "For José Angel Valente, the poet is one who must brave the shadows of the unknown, like the mystic who loses himself and is reborn in the Beloved; like Lazarus, victorious over death yet knowing that death will come again; like the rooster rupturing the limits of the night" (167–68). Frequently in Valente's works poetry is associated with potential illumination. See, for example, the untitled poem that begins with the line "Objetos de la noche" (Objects of the night) and "Palabra" (Word), both from *Material memoria (1977–78)* (*Punto cero* 461; 464). See Hart ("Metapoetic Texts" and "Poetry and Language"); Persin ("Poem as Process"); Sherno; and Ugalde for studies advancing this view.

14. Valente observes: "La poesía es importante, incluso las personas más profanas tienen necesidad de ella, porque la poesía es una invitación a una meditación profunda de la palabra, y como lo que realmente tenemos es la palabra, te incitan a lo más esencial, a todo el depósito de cosas que hay en la palabra, que es lo que nos hace reaccionar y vivir" (Poetry is important, even the most worldly of people need it, because poetry is an invitation to deep meditation on the word, and since what we really have is the word, it stimulates you to the most essential, to the entire depository of things that there are in the word, that is what makes us respond and live) (*El País* 1988, 22). It is in both this "meditation" and this "depository" where *différance* comes into play. In viewing decon-

structive reading, Johnson explains: "sometimes the discrepancy is produced . . . by a double-edged word, which serves as a hinge that both articulates and breaks open the explicit statement being made" ("Introduction" xiv). Moreover, as Derrida has shown, the text, thus, not only functions against its own assertions but also inscribes a *"systematic* "other message" behind or through what is being said" (Johnson, "Introduction" xiii). When examining Valente's poetry Debicki points out, "If the writing of a text is a progressive act of discovery and if a word's meaning is evolving gradually, then language is never fully in the author's power and the process of writing is a dialectical confrontation between poet and language" (*PD* 103). This observation could well be applied to "Primer poema." However, the confrontation between poet and language exists not only because, as Debicki claims, "language is never fully in the author's power," but also because there is in language the "conflictuality of *différance*" that, as Derrida explains, "can never be totally resolved" (*POS* 44). Valente describes the heterodox and contradictory nature of language in another of his poems, "Como una invitación o una súplica" (Like an invitation or a plea) from *La memoria de los signos (1960–65)* (The memory of the signs), in this way:

> En vano vuelven las palabras
> pues ellas mismas todavía esperan
> la mano que las quiebre y las vacíe
> hasta hacerlas ininteligibles y puras
> para que de ellas nazca un sentido distinto,
> incomprensible y claro.   (lines 21–26, *Punto cero* 223)

> In vain the words return
> then they themselves still await
> that hand that breaks them and empties them
> until they are made unintelligible and pure
> so that they may be born with a different meaning,
> incomprehensible and clear.

15. "Esplendor negro" has attracted critical attention because most critics view it as a fundamental text of *Insistencias en Luzbel*. Sanz Echevarría, for example, in examining mystic allusions in *Insistencias en Luzbel*, sees the metaphoric "Esplendor negro," the central image of the poem, as an example of the "mística de la nada" (mystic of nothingness) (36, 41) characterizing this collection. Benson examines "Esplendor negro," stressing both the allegorical allusions to mysticism and also the speaker's "search for his own method of expression" ("Memory" 323). Amusco, commenting on both the poet and on lines 22–23 of the poem, observes: "El vacío anulador que él adivina, ese 'Esplendor negro' que columbra tras el ser, no le atrae con apremiamente rapto; todo lo contrario: le repele, le espanta" (The annuling void that he predicts, that 'Black splendor' that is perceived to follow being, does not attract him with urgent rapture; quite the contrary: it repulses him, it terrifies him) ("Estética" 12). Persin discusses the collection, in general, and this poem, in particular, from the perspective of the poet's desire "to call into question language's power to communicate" (*RSP* 48). For Bradford, the three poems comprising the first section of *Insistencias en Luzbel*, of which "Esplendor negro" is one, are texts that "focus on the speaker's attempt to imagine nothingness and to define himself in light of it" ("Dialectic" 2–3). She views the title of this poem as "the poetic symbol of the void" (3). Jiménez agrees with Bradford, claiming that in "Esplendor negro," "Invitación a un blanco mantel" (Invitation to a white tablecloth), and "Entendimiento de una experiencia" (Understanding an experience) we see "la concreción poética, hasta donde el humano lenguaje lo permita, de la Nada" (the poetic con-

cretion, as far as human language permits, of Nothingness) ("Esplendor y apagamiento" 16). Of these same three poems, and of the collection in general, Villena observes that Brines is trying to "Contar lo incontable: la muerte, la aniquilación, la nada" (To describe the indescribable: death, annihilation, nothingness) ("Sobre *IEL*" 217). The critical bibliography of Brines's poetry is lengthy. See note 1 of my Introduction where I discuss those critical works most influential to my readings.

16. Persin observes, "The use of the *tú* form of address reinforces the ambiguity of the text. The poet's *tú* may address at once his own poetic persona, the reader who joins him in the metaphysical and metapoetic quest, and Satan, who has fallen from the light" (*RSP* 48).

17. Brines reconstructs his own theory of illumination, drawing on the intertextual context of Plato and Augustine, among others. In Plato's thought, for example, Illumination played an active part.

> Plato, like many other thinkers, prophets and mystics, spoke readily of the sudden flash of understanding or insight in the mind as a flood of light (see, for example, his Seventh Letter, 341C, 344B). The image is, indeed, one that occurs naturally in many languages and is especially apt for the description of insight thought to have been achieved as a result of external aid of some kind, of an 'inspiration.' The language of inspiration is based on the entry of breath, and that of illumination on the entry of light into the mind. The Stoic tradition can be said to have developed the former analogy in its metaphysics; Plato was undoubtedly the father of the philosophical tradition to which the analogy of light is fundamental. In his *Republic,* Plato employed the analogy of light and vision to describe the process of understanding or of knowledge in general (Books V–VIII). . . . In Christian thought it is in the work of St. Augustine of Hippo that the theory of illumination is found in its most highly developed form. Like Plato, Augustine thought of understanding as analogous to seeing. Understanding, or intellectual sight, was therefore, he held, conditional on illumination, just as physical sight was; only here the light was the intelligible light that emanated from the divine mind and in illuminating the mind endowed it with understanding. Understanding, in the last resort, was an inward participation of the human mind in the divine." (Markus 129–30)

18. "The Greek noun *logos*, derived from the root found in the verb *lego*, 'I say,' in the classical period covered a wide range of meanings expressed by quite different words in most modern languages. Thus, word, speech, argument, explanation, doctrine, esteem, numerical computation, measure, proportion, plea, principle, and reason (whether human or divine)—all represent standard meanings of the one Greek word" (Kerferd 83).

19. Persin sees it this way: "the speaker is caught in a paradox of sorts. He has arrived at the perplexing conclusion that language is insufficient, yet he must continue to submit himself to its nebulous and shifting demands. In his search for absolute knowledge, the perfect one-to-one correspondence between the thing and its name, the poet, like Satan, falls into the abyss" (*RSP* 49).

20. This reading of "Esplendor negro" is sustained by other poems of *Insistencias en Luzbel*. See, for example, "El curso de la luz" (The course of light) (*ED* 205), "Otra vez Fausto" (Once again Faust) (*ED* 223), "Noche de la desposesión" (Night of the dispossession) (*ED* 225–26), "Palabras desde una pausa" (Words from a pause) (*ED* 241), and "El porqué de las palabras" (The reason for words) (*ED* 241–42).

21. The Spanish infinitive *poder* is derived from the vulgar Latin *potere*, itself a substitute for the classical Latin *posse*, which is a contracted form of *potis esse*, *ser capaz* (to be able) (*DCE* 588). In Spanish, the verb *poder*, the nouns *poder, potencia* (power,

ability), *potestad* (power, dominion), and the adjectives *poderoso* (powerful) and *potencial* (potential, possible), for example, all have the same etymological source.

22. J. Hillis Miller points out in "Stevens' Rock and Criticism as Cure" that "Catachresis is the violent, forced, or abusive use of a word to name something which has no literal name . . . Catachresis explodes the distinction between literal and figurative on which the analysis of tropes is based and so leads the 'science' of rhetoric to destroy itself as science, as clear and distinct knowledge of truth" (II, 28). *The Princeton Encyclopedia of Poetry and Poetics* defines catachresis as "the misapplication of a word, especially in a strained or mixed metaphor or in an implied metaphor. It need not be a ridiculous misapplication as in bad poetry, but may be a deliberate wresting of a term from its normal and proper significance" (104). Arthur Quinn offers another definition for "the most problematic of metonymies" (55). He explains catachresis as the "Apparently inappropriate substitution of one word for another, inappropriate because there is not an obviously definable relationship between the two" (102).

23. As Johnson explains in the "Translator's Introduction" to Derrida's *Dissemination*, "A and B are no longer opposed, nor are they equivalent. Indeed, they are no longer even equivalent to themselves. They are their own differance from themselves" (xiii).

24. It is worthwhile to recall J. Hillis Miller's insightful observations in "The Critic as Host": "The critic's attempt to untwist the elements in the text he interprets only twists them up again in another place and leaves always a remnant of opacity, or an added opacity, as yet unraveled. . . . The critic cannot unscramble the tangle of lines of meaning, comb its threads out so they shine clearly side by side. He can only retrace the text, set its elements in motion once more, in that experience of the failure of determinable reading which is decisive here" (247–48). De Man looks at deconstructive readings as those that can only repeat what "caused the error in the first place. They leave a margin of error, a residue of logical tension that prevents the closure of the deconstructive discourse and accounts for its narrative and allegorical mode" (*Allegories* 242).

25. Derrida points out: "Dissemination, . . . although producing a nonfinite number of semantic effects, can be led back neither to a present of simple origin . . . nor to an eschatological presence. It marks an irreducible and generative multiplicity. The supplement and the turbulence of a certain lack fracture the limit of the text, forbidding an exhaustive and closed formalization of it, or at least a saturating taxonomy of its themes, its signified, its meanings" (*POS* 45).

Chapter 2. (Un)Tangling "The Weave of Time"

1. A number of critics have examined the theme of time in Brines's poetry. Soon after the publication of *Las brasas* in 1960, Jiménez characterized the collection as follows: "ese centro espiritual desde el cual se ha conformado el libro de Brines parece ser *la serenidad resignada con que se contempla y medita el paso del tiempo, pero siempre desde dentro y a lo largo de una existencia humana intransferible*" (that spiritual center within which Brines's collection fits seems to be the resigned serenity with which *the passage of time is contemplated, but always from within and during non-transferable human existence*) (*Cinco poetas* 419). These perceptive observations served to predict a theme that was to dominate Brines's poetry of the next three decades. In Bousoño's cornerstone article examining Brines's poetry from 1960–71, "Situación y características de la poesía de Francisco Brines," the critic studies various stylistic techniques (temporal superimpositions, temporal juxtapositions, etc.) used by the poet in order to create his poetic vision of "la temporalidad y precariedad de la vida y del mundo" (the temporality and precari-

ousness of life and of the world) (52). Cañas's recent anthology of many of Brines's poems exploring the theme of time explains in his Introduction to *El rumor del tiempo*: "En verdad, una aguda conciencia del paso del tiempo es el atributo principal del joven poeta que aparece en su obra. Este protagonista es un solitario que reflexiona desde temprana edad sobre la vejez, la muerte y la nada" (Really, an acute awareness of the passage of time that appears in his work is the principal attribute of the young poet. This protagonist is a solitary one who reflects on old age, death and nothingness from a very early age) (9). Looking briefly at a few other critical works, Villar Ribot's recent essay studies, what he terms, "La mirada del tiempo" (The gaze of time) in Brines's 1986 collection, *El otoño de las rosas*. Persin's 1987 study examines what she terms "the illusory nature of temporal existence" in a few specific poems of *Insistensias en Luzbel* demonstrating that "Although Brines's poetry clearly mirrors the metaphysical and artistic preoccupations of its author, it also has the power to communicate and create for the reader the experiences of pain, paradox, uncertainty, mystery, and hope of daily existence" (*RSP* 64). In Debicki's 1982 "Francisco Brines: Text and Reader," the critic investigates the theme of the passing of time in *Las brasas,* demonstrating that "the devices of a text interplay with the reader's expectations to produce an unusual and significant experience" (*PD* 21). Luis Antonio de Villena's 1975 *Insula* article underscores that time is one of the "constants" (4) in Brines's poetry. Examining Brines's poetry of his first three collections, he further notes, "El tiempo . . . en su pasar, va haciendo del hombre un ser más experto en la reflexión y más pobre en su relación con la vida. El tiempo nos convierte en menesterosos. Su paso nos agobia en todo momento, porque nos dice que la felicidad, la belleza, el amor o el deseo no son perdurables y están amenazados por el final irrevocable (causa del tiempo) que es sombra, noche y ceniza" (Time . . . in its passing, makes humankind a being who is more skilled in reflection and more wretched in relationship to life. Time converts us into needy beings. Its passage overwhelms us in every moment, because it tells us that happiness, beauty, love or desire are not everlasting and thus are threatened by the irrevocable end [the cause of time] that is shadow, night and ash) (4).

2. The Spanish noun *trama* does not convey a singular "meaning." I have opted to translate it here as "woof" in an attempt not only to thread my way through Brines's temporal-textual-existential "weave" but also to continue to intertangle my own critical text in this "weave." An etymological retracing of the noun *trama* leads, however, to differing, semantic, forking paths, thus problematizing the work of translation.

3. Heraclitus contends that "all change can be regarded as that between opposites" and when opposites are "taken together" a "unity" results. See *The Pre-Socratic Philosophers*, especially pp. 191–93.

4. See my earlier article, "Francisco Brines's *Aún no*: Poetry as Knowledge," where I analyze in detail the poem "Noche" and discuss the unity of symbolic opposites in Brines's poetry. Some of the observations expressed in this chapter had their origin in this earlier piece. At the time of the publication of that article, however, I was still searching for and, in fact, believed I would find eventually unequivocal "meaning" in both poetry and criticism written about poetry. Time as change, time as mysteriously slipping away, time as a continuous passing away is apparent in many of the observations of the first-person speaker of *Aún no*. For example, in "Extinción" this speaker affirms: "Sólo soy un suspiro, que dice su extinción" (I am only a sigh, that speaks its extinction) (line 1) and in "Sombrío ardor" the speaker observes: "Rueda el tiempo / por las sordas paredes de este cuarto, / y siento que la vida se deshace" (Time wanders about / through the still walls of this room, / and I sense that life vanishes) (lines 12–14).

5. See Benson's "Memory, Tradition and the Reader in the Poetry of Francisco Brines" where the critic studies memory as the "Leitmotiv of his work, the subject of endless variations and experiences" (308).

6. I study "Al lector" in detail, utilizing a reader-oriented critical approach, in "Writing and Reading: Dialectical Correlatives in Francisco Brines' *Insistencias en Luzbel*."

7. See Benson's "El amor contra la nada: Pedro Salinas, Francisco Brines y la tradición clásica española" for a recent study of this theme in Brines's poetry.

8. In "Retracing the Text: Francisco Brines's *Poemas excluidos*," I carefully scrutinize this poem. It is to be noted that this poem would have formed a part of *Las brasas*, at least the second edition of this collection published by Hontanar. At the time of the initial publication of *Las brasas*, however, the poet could not find the text and thus it remained excluded from the collection only to be "recovered," to use Brines's term, later, and then included in *Poemas excluidos*. See Brines's accompanying commentary to this poem (*PE* 38–39).

9. J. Hillis Miller discusses the problems arising when the critic attempts to unknot or simplify "the problems of narrative form" in his article "Ariadne's Thread: Repetition and the Narrative Line" (6–61). Some fifteen years after its publication, this article inspired, in part, the discussion of the problems confronting this critic when entering the temporal tangle of Brines's poetry. Miller asks:

> What line should the critic follow in explicating, unfolding, or unknotting these passages? [referring to passages by Ruskin, Gaskell, Pater]. How should he thread his way into the labyrinthine problems of narrative form, and in particular into the problem of repetition in fiction? The line of the line itself? The motif, image, concept, or formal model of the line, however, far from being a 'clue' to the labyrinth, turns out, as the passage from Ruskin suggests, to be itself the labyrinth. To follow the motif of the line will not simplify the knotted problems of narrative form but to retrace the whole tangle from the starting place of a certain point of entry. (60–61)

10. In the Preface to *The Linguistic Moment,* J. Hillis Miller writes, "This preface, as I have said, comes first but was written last. It is placed at the beginning for the reader of the book, at its end for the author. The reading of the book, the traversal of the never quite complete circling it makes, will bring the reader back to where he or she is at the beginning. At the beginning, nevertheless, the reader is not quite able to know where he or she is, or it would not be necessary to read the book to get there with a new awareness" (xvii).

11. According to Mundle, "Most philosophers would now agree with [William] James that time is a notion that we construct from temporal relations which are sense given. Such philosophers must surely accept the thesis that temporal relations are sense given *within* the present and that this duration of which we are 'incessantly sensible' ought to be called 'the *conscious* present.' [E. R.] Clay and James called this duration 'the specious [that is, pseudo] present' because they assumed that only its later boundary should be called 'the real present'" (138).

12. In the Introduction to *Selección propia*, Brines observes:

> Hay muchas maneras de situarse el poeta ante la poesía, y pienso que, en mi caso, mucho tiene que ver la mía con lo que ante ella experimenté en mis años adolescentes. Mis primeros poemas, a pesar de su exagerada mediocridad, me depararon una experiencia mágica: supongo que entonces sólo comparable al uso sexual del cuerpo, si el hallazgo de un tan refinado placer hubiera conllevado la creación de una criatura deseada. Pero esta última experiencia no fue vivida por mí. Así que, situado el muchacho ante el papel blanco, fluía, como un prodigio, el acontecer de las palabras, y tan peregrina acción iba acompañada de un gran placer nunca antes

conocido, con el final resultado de la misteriosa aparición de un cuerpo, a mi pare-
cer, exactísimo. La emoción que allí se me entregaba como ajena, me pertenecía:
yo era a la vez la fuente y el sediento. (15–16) (There are many ways that the poet
situates himself with respect to his poetry, and I think that, in my case, a great deal
has to do with what I experienced with respect to my poetry in my adolescent years.
My first poems, despite their exaggerated mediocrity, offered me a magical experience: I suppose then comparable only to the sexuality of the body, when the refined
pleasure of this finding might have assisted in the creation of a desired creature. But
this last experience was not lived by me. Thus, the young boy situated with respect
to the white paper, from whom would flow, like a prodigy, the occurrence of words,
and such a peregrine action would be accompanied by a great pleasure never before
known, with the final result of the mysterious appearance of a body, it seemed to
me, very exact. The emotion to which I surrendered myself as if it were another's,
pertained to me: I was simultaneously both the spring and the thirsty one.)

13. Moliner defines *ahora* in this way: "El momento en que se habla se expresa con
'ahora, ahora mismo, en este [en este preciso] momento, en estos momentos, en este [en
este preciso] instante, en estos [en estos precisos] instantes'" (The moment in which one
speaks one expresses with 'at this moment, right now, in this [in this very] moment, in
these moments, in this [in this very] instant, in these [in these very] instants' (Vol. 2,
1308).

14. According to Moliner in the *Diccionario del uso del español*, the Spanish word
presente is derived from the Latin *praesens, -entis*, the present participle of *praeesse*. "Se
aplica al tiempo en que está cuando se habla, a los acontecimientos que ocurren en él y
a los tiempos verbales que se refieren a él" (It is applied to the time in which one is when
one speaks, to the events occurring in it and to the verbal tenses that refer to it) (Vol. 2,
834). The Latin root *prae + esse*, "to be before," "to be at hand," hence *praesens, prae-
sent -em*, "present," "immediate," "prompt" (*OED* 2285), is of importance in my discussion of Brines's poem.

15. *Harper's Latin Dictionary* defines *creatura* as "creature, thing created" (178).
The Spanish verb *crear* was derived from the Latin *creare*, according to Moliner (Vol.
1, 797). Of the noun *criatura* Moliner observes: "(1) Con relación a Dios, cualquier cosa
creada. Particularmente, los seres animados. (2) Niño pequeño. También considerado en
el seno de la madre" ([1] With respect to God, any created thing. Particularly, animate
beings. [2] Small child. Also considered in the womb of the mother) (Vol. 1, 802). Both
the Spanish *crear, criatura* and the Latin *creare, creatura* have at their origin the Greek
root *poe-*, as noted by Moliner (Vol. 1, 798). Moliner also points out that the Spanish
noun *poeta* was derived from the Greek *poietes*, which, in turn, was derived from the
Greek *poieo*, to create (Vol. 2, 792). Citing Corominas, the Spanish noun *poeta*, was
derived from the Latin *poeta*, which, in turn, was derived from the Greek ποιητής
"maker," "creator," "author" (*DCE*, Vol. 4, 589).

16. As Harvey points out,

Derrida insists that the *now* is fundamentally non-existent, it is a constituted moment
of time which essentially is non-temporal. In a certain respect, he is applying the
investigations of the Husserlian notions of time to the tradition of metaphysics as a
whole. What this entails is a recognition of a fundamental absence within the
moment of the present. That is, with the movement of consciousness from retention
to protention, and back again, we have a result that is synthetic which forms that
which metaphysics calls the now: the Present. This essential moment for the understanding of truth is internally divided and essentially so. It is always a 'recollection'

of the past, albeit 'held' in consciousness, and a movement toward the non-yet-present future (120). See Mundle's discussion of "Consciousness of Time" in *The Encyclopedia of Philosophy* (Vol. 8, 134–39), where William James's observations regarding the perception of time are summarized. In brief, James's concept of the "specious present," a term invented by E. R. Clay, views time as a line of which the specious present is a segment whose later boundary is the real present. Both James and Clay conclude that "the specious present and its contents are really past" (Mundle 135). James held that "we are continuously directly perceiving or intuiting a past duration and its contents" (Mundle 135).

17. In the Introduction to *Selección propia,* Brines writes of "el acto de la unión carnal" (the act of carnal union) affirming: "El acto sexual ha roto repetidamente barreras de clase, razas, edades y aun de los sexos mismos. Y lo ha hecho arrostrando mil calamidades, de este mundo o del otro, en una imperiosa necesidad de afirmar la vida en contra de lo que la niega" (The sexual act has repeatedly broken class, race and age barriers and even those pertaining to gender itself. And it has done it defying a thousand misfortunes both of this world and the next, with an imperious need to affirm life against all that negates it) (48).

18. Of course, in "Ariadne's Thread" J. Hillis Miller brilliantly deconstructs this view of "narrative line," where narrative event follows narrative event, when he ravels and unravels "the image of the line" in this article. See page 72, in particular.

19. According to Corominas, the Spanish *azahar* is from the "hispanoárabe *zahar* (ar. *zahr* 'flor en general' flor de azahar,' de la raíz *z-h-r* 'lucir,' 'ser hermoso', (florecer')" (hispanic-arabic *zahar* (ar. *zahr* "flower in general," "flower of citrus trees," from the root *z-h-r* "to shine," "to be beautiful," "to flower") (*DCE*, Vol. 1, 431).

20. Other poems in which Elca can be found include "Yo no era el mejor" (I was not the best), which carries the comment "(*Tarde de verano en Elca*)" ([*Summer afternoon in Elca*]), (*PO, ED* 60) and "Los ocios ganados" (Acquired pastimes) (*OR* 10).

21. The Spanish noun *sepulturero* is defined as "El que tiene por oficio abrir las sepulturas y sepultar a los muertos" (*DLE* 1195) (He whose job it is to open graves and bury the dead).

22. *Harpers Latin Dictionary* defines *conscientia* as "a knowing of a thing together with another person, joint knowledge, consciousness" (426). The *Oxford Latin Dictionary* defines *conscientia* as follows: "1 The holding of knowledge in common. 2 the fact of being privy to a crime, complicity. 2 The act of being aware of something one has done or is responsible for, consciousness. b private knowledge (of external matters). 3 (w. animi, w. mentis, or alone) An inward perception of the rectitude or otherwise of one's actions, moral sense, conscience" (411).

23. The symbolic penumbra figures in many of Brines's poems of the last three decades. See "Junto a la mesa se ha quedado solo" (He has remained alone near the table) (*ED* 23–24), "El barranco de los pájaros" (The precipice of the birds) (*ED* 29–32), "La vieja ley" (The old law) (*ED* 57–58), "Balcón en sombra" (Balcony in shadow) (*ED* 117–19), "Relato superviviente" (Surviving report) (*ED* 129–33), "Los signos de la madrugada" (The signs of dawn) (*ED* 159), "La realidad no permanece" (Reality does not last) (*ED* 233), "Sucesión de mi mismo" (Succession of my self) (*ED* 236–37), "Ultimo encuentro de los tres" (The last meeting of the three) (*ED* 237), "El huésped" (The guest) (*OR* 23), "Erótica secreta de los iguales" (The secret erotic poetry of two equals) (*OR* 31–32), among others.

24. Jiménez provides a lengthy stylistic analysis of this poem in *Cinco poetas del tiempo* (424–42). Some years later he offers a brief synopsis of this same poem's major themes in relation to the "proceso de extinción" (process of extinction) that is *Las brasas*

("Esplendor y apagamiento" 11). Debicki's observations in "Francisco Brines: Text and Reader" focus on the reader's collaborative role in "Está en penumbra el cuarto" (*PD* 21–25).

25. The Parcae, as the weavers of humankind's life, immediately come to mind. Cirlot points out, "The act of weaving represents, basically, creation and life, and particularly the latter in so far as it denotes accumulation and multiplication or growth" (369).

Chapter 3. Differing Substitutions: Naming "la nada"

1. When reading Derrida Harvey points out: "The name is the locus not only of language but also of Reason, *Logos*, and metaphysics as such. It is for 'being-in-search-of-a-name' that Derrida reproaches Heidegger and the latter's reliance on the notions of the proper and the essential in his 'overturning' of humanism as such. It is the structure of authority and power of the 'proper' that Derrida hopes to (a) reveal and (b) escape from or overcome" (211).

2. This is the view argued in my earlier article "Modos de ser en *Insistencias en Luzbel* de Francisco Brines" (36–37). There I attempted to determine the "meaning" of this poem.

3. Spivak points out that the notion of play is important. She observes, citing Derrida: "Knowledge is not a systematic tracking down of a truth that is hidden but may be found. It is rather the field 'of freeplay, that is to say, a field of infinite substitutions in the closure of a finite ensemble'" (xix; Derrida's observation is from *L'Ecriture et la différence* 423, as cited by Spivak). Explicating the Derridean strategy of writing "sous rature" Spivak observes: "In examining familiar things we come to such unfamiliar conclusions that our very language is twisted and bent even as it guides us. Writing 'under erasure' is the mark of this contortion" (xiv). Later, Spivak further states: "the name of this gesture effacing the presence of a thing and yet keeping it legible, in Derrida's lexicon, is 'writing,'—the gesture that both frees us from and guards us within, the metaphysical enclosures" (xli).

4. It could be argued that various Existentialist pre-texts underlie Brines's multiple namings of "la nada" in this poem and in others of *Insistencias en Luzbel*, in particular. Throughout my "Modos de ser" I investigate various textual affiliations with Existentialist thought, particularly that of Heidegger, Sartre, and Kierkegaard, in this collection. Bradford ("Dialectic" 1) and Amusco ("Estética" 1, 12) also look at possible Existentialist intertexts for Brines's collection.

5. Cañas sees this poem and this concept in this way: "Pero la nada aparece cuando se interrumpe el tiempo humano, a la vez que lo sostiene desde sus (posibles) comienzos. De hecho, es ahí donde parecería residir la clave de este concepto en Brines: la nada es sólo la conciencia de la terminación arbitraria del tiempo personal. Por lo tanto, la nada sólo puede ser el destino último, pero también anterior, de nuestro tiempo individual" (But nothingness appears when human time is interrupted, while sustaining it from its (possible) beginnings. In fact, it is there where the key to this concept in Brines's poetry would seem to reside: nothingness is only consciousness of the arbitrary termination of personal time. For that reason, nothingness can only be the final, but also anterior, destiny of our individual time) (Introduction, *El rumor del tiempo* 16–17).

6. I argue this point in "Modos de ser en *Insistencias en Luzbel*" (37), although there I arrive at a different conclusion.

7. Spivak observes of *différance*: "Each substitution is also a displacement, and carries a different metaphoric charge, as Derrida reminds us often" (lxx).

8. Bradford reaches a similar conclusion, observing that for Brines "language is deficient in its failure to reveal the causes of existence" ("Two Recent Approaches" 38). Persin studies Brines's poem, discussing what she terms "the metaphysical void of human existence" and how this void is characterized "by the very language of his text" (*RSP* 51). She concludes, "The poet's never-ending search for adequate expression exemplifies, represents, and describes the search for existential truth on a universal level. For him, there can be no difference" (*RSP* 51).

9. Spivak notes: "Derrida, questioning the unity of language itself, and putting metaphor under erasure, radically opens up textuality" (lxxiv).

10. Persin reaches a similar conclusion regarding the elusive subject of the verb *niega* (*RSP* 51), although she arrives at a different interpretation of the poem.

11. Harvey's observations are worthy of note:

It is thus no accident that Derrida uses the term '*différance*,' which is not a 'proper' term. '*Différance*,' as a word, does not properly speaking exist; neither does *différance* as such for Derrida. We have thus a good example of what Derrida calls the inextricable relation of signifier and signified, at the same time as we have a description of that process. *Différance* is both signifier and signified here. One can also realize in this 'example' the structure of *différance* as such as the economy which produces the same, the name, and the proper, but which itself is none of these. *Différance* is a composite term made up of the two proper words: to differ and to defer . . . , and together for Derrida they form *différance* (the ending being better translated perhaps as differ*ing* in English). The problem, however, is that the essential impropriety of '*différance*' is therein lost since 'differing' is a quite appropriately recognized official word. Nevertheless 'differing' sustains the notion of the process of movement which Derrida aims to describe here. But the movement is a sort of oscillation more than a unilateral, or one-dimensional, uni-directional process. Indeed it is the movement between the thought of differing and deferring: the former being related to spatiality, the latter to temporality. Both include a notion of opening, of a promise, of an extension, of a postponement, of a detour, of a repetition, of a substitution, of a representation, and indeed of a sort of *doubling* that exists over the extension of space and time. But the two terms nevertheless, in spite of this apparent commonality of root, cannot be collapsed into one whole without the *eclipsing* of one aspect by the other. If one thinks of differing, the notion of spatiality is brought into mind; if one thinks of deferring, likewise for the notion of temporality. But the two juxtaposed within one concept leave one impotent to consider both simultaneously. Instead, phenomenologically, what seems to occur is a vibration, or oscillation back and forth between one and the other. As one comes into view, the other recedes into the background, and vice versa. This is precisely what Derrida names *différance*—in all senses of the term. (210)

12. Derrida refers to the "theme of supplementarity" that "tells us in a text what a text is, it tells us in writing what writing is" (*OG* 163).

13. The allusion to Atkins's "The Story of Error" (*RD* 79–88) is intentional.

14. Brines, in a way, is recalling, even renaming, the Heideggerian notion of the *Verfallen*. See my "Modos de ser en *Insistencias en Luzbel*" (43–44; 54–55). I have opted to translate "olvido" as "forgetfulness" due to this earlier study of ontological modes evidenced in this collection.

15. Perhaps the poetic voices heard throughout *Insistencias en Luzbel* are describing and redescribing the poet's act of writing "sous rature." Derrida, in describing writing, recalls: "At each step I was obliged to proceed by ellipses, corrections and correc-

tions of corrections, letting go of each concept at the very moment I needed to use it" ("The Original Discussion of '*Différance*' (1968)," which took place after his Address of January 27 now reproduced in *Derrida and Différance* [84]).

16. *A Dictionary of Angels* notes that the word *angel* "derives from *angiras* (Sanskrit), a divine spirit; from the Persian *angaros*, a courier; from the Greek *angelos*, meaning a messenger" (20). See *A Dictionary of the Bible* (32–33) for the activity and functions of angels.

17. See my "Modos de ser" (42–48).

18. Brines's observation is quoted by Jiménez in "Esplendor y apagamiento" (18).

19. I too offer another differing reading in my earlier "Modos de ser" where I attempt to decipher the myth of existence and the enigmatic figure of "Luzbel" (see pp. 49–51, in particular). There I observe:

> After evoking the traditional mythology associated with the Angel, Lucifer, and God, Brines suddenly discloses his own mythicizing version of each figure. Consequently, each is recreated within the personal myth the poet seeks to disclose in the mythopoems of *Insistencias en Luzbel*. The plot of the Lucifer prologue is not associated with the Judeo-Christian lore of the Angel, Lucifer and God. This myth, rather, conceals the philosophical, existential and metaphorical ideas developed by the poet in his explanation of the meaning of the modes of authentic/inauthentic Being.

I go on to argue: "Unable to accept fully the ontological possibility of non-Being, the poet's protagonists listen to and befriend the tempter, 'Luzbel-olvido'. The prophetic combat of the epigraphic 'Variación I' becomes a part of man's own existence as he seeks to forget 'la nada' and becomes an extension of 'el olvido' embodied by Lucifer: 'Todos somos la espada de Luzbel'" (50). Benson offers yet another interpretation. He investigates various literary allusions in *Insistencias en Luzbel* and provides an insightful reading of the first epigraph of the collection where the mysterious figure of "el negro Caballero del olvido" (the black Knight of forgetfulness) is viewed as a traditional representation of death and also as a reference to Satan of the title. He asks, "Cuál de nosotros no ha oído de niño que Luzbel nos llega 'callada y cautelosamente?'" (Which of us has not heard since childhood that Lucifer comes to us "silently and cautiously") ("Convenciones" 3). Looking briefly at another reading offered by Sanz Echevarría we find: "'Descifremos el mito,' como escribe Brines en el mismo poema: el hombre nace inmortal porque, en su inocencia, cree en un Dios como garantía de la eternidad de todo lo existente; más adelante se dará cuenta de la 'devastación' a que nos somete el tiempo de que no hay nadie más poderoso que él; al ser Dios un engaño, también la vida se transforma en otro tanto" ("Let us decipher the myth," as Brines writes in this same poem: man is born immortal because, in his innocence, he believes in God as a guarantee of eternity and of all that exists; a little farther on he will realize the "devastation" to which time subjects us and that there is no one more powerful than he; when God is deceit, life is also transformed into another) (42).

20. *A Dictionary of Angels* further explains: "It should be pointed out that the authors of the books of the Old Testament knew nothing of fallen angels, and do not mention them, although, at times, as in Job 4:18, the Lord 'put no trust' in his angels and 'charged them with folly,' which would indicate that angels were not all they should be. The name *Lucifer* was applied to Satan by St. Jerome and other Church Fathers. Milton in *Paradise Lost* applied the name to the demon of sinful pride" (176).

21. *A Dictionary of Angels* points out that allusively, "lucifer" has become the designation for one who commits the sin of Lucifer, in other words, one who commits the

sin of pride or ambition (112). Moreover, "In Numbers 22:22 the angel of the Lord stands against Balaam 'for adversary' (satan). In other Old Testament books (Job, I Chronicles, Psalms, Zechariah) the term likewise designates an office; and the angel investing that office is not apostate or fallen. He becomes such starting in early New Testament times and writings, when he emerges as Satan (capital S), the prince of evil and enemy of God, and is characterized by such titles as 'prince of this world' (John 16:11) and 'prince of the power of the air' (Ephesians 2: 2)" (261). *A Dictionary of the Bible* notes, "The term *Satan* is Hebrew and means 'adversary'" (888).

22. By interrogating the medium employed, the writer cannot reduce the language of the text to a single, precise determination. Rather, writer, be she/he poet or critic, always already is engaged in the act, the strategy of learning, as Spivak observes, "to use and erase our language at the same time" (xviii). Spivak further notes: "It is the strategy of using the only available language while not subscribing to its premises, or 'operat[ing] according to the vocabulary of the very thing that one delimits'" (xviii, where the critic cites Derrida, *Margins of Philosophy* 18). Harvey sees it this way: "Writing, we should recall, is the condition of the possibility of language, but it is therefore also a certain condition of impossibility" (150).

23. Bradford offers a reading of "Entendimiento de una experiencia" ("Dialectic" 6–9). Also see Sanz Echevarría (36).

24. Regarding the search for a semantic center, J. Hillis Miller observes in "Stevens' Rock and Criticism as Cure": "The origin rather is bifurcated, even trifurcated, a forking root which leads the searcher for the ground of the word into the labyrinthine wanderings in the forest of words. . . . However hard he [the critic] tries to fix the word in a single sense it remains indeterminable, uncannily resisting his attempts to end its movement" (I, 11).

25. Derrida observes, "Thus one could consider all the pairs of opposites on which philosophy is constructed and on which our discourse lives, not in order to see opposition erase itself but to see what indicates that each of the terms must appear as the *différance* of the other, as the other different and deferred in the economy of the same" (*DIF* 17).

Afterword

1. Of the deconstructive enterprise Spivak explains in the "Translator's Preface" to *Of Grammatology*: "Deconstruction seems to offer a way out of the closure of knowledge. By inaugurating the open-ended indefiniteness of textuality—by thus 'placing in the abyss' (*mettre en abime*), as the French expression would have it—it shows us the lure of the abyss as freedom. The fall into the abyss of deconstruction inspires us with as much pleasure as fear. We are intoxicated by the prospect of never hitting bottom." She further observes: "Thus a further deconstruction deconstructs deconstruction, both as the search for a foundation (the critic behaving as if she means what she says in her text), and as the pleasure of the bottomless. The tool for this, as indeed for any deconstruction, is our desire, itself a deconstructive and grammatological structure that forever differs from (we only desire what is not ourselves) and defers (desire is never fulfilled) the text of ourselves" (lxxvii). Anderson characterizes the deconstructive, interpretive act in this way: "Although to write we must provisionally assume that we know what we mean as critics, discourse is always already caught up in the warring forces within our own critical text, the play of differences within the critical text that both allows us to write and guarantees its deconstructability" (150–51).

Works Cited

Aldrich, Mark. "A Poetics of Search of Paradox: The Poetry of Francisco Brines," Ph.D. diss., University of Massachusetts, 1990.

Alvardo Tenorio, Harold. *La poesía española contemporánea. Cinco poetas de la generación del Cincuenta: Angel González, José María Caballero Bonald, Carlos Barral, Jaime Gil de Biedma, y Francisco Brines.* Bogotá: Editorial La Oveja Negra, n.d.

Amusco, Alejandro. "Algunos aspectos de la obra poética de Francisco Brines." *Cuadernos Hispanoamericanos* 346 (1979): 52–74.

———. "Francisco Brines: estética de la nada y del sufrimiento." *Insula* 376 (1978): 1, 12.

Anderson, Danny. "Deconstruction: Critical Strategy/Strategic Criticism." In *Contemporary Literary Theory,* edited by G. Douglas Atkins and Laura Morrow. Amherst: The University of Massachusetts Press, 1989.

Atkins, G. Douglas. *Reading Deconstruction. Deconstructive Reading.* Lexington: The University Press of Kentucky, 1983.

Badosa, Enrique. "Primero hablemos de Júpiter (la poesía como medio de conocimiento)." *Papeles de Son Armadans* 10 (1958): 32–46 and 135–59.

Batlló, José. *Antología de la nueva poesía española.* Madrid: El Bardo, 1968.

Benson, Douglas K. "El amor contra la nada: Pedro Salinas, Francisco Brines y la tradición clásica española." *Revista Canadiense de Estudios Hispánicos* 15.1 (Fall 1990): 1–18.

———. "Convenciones de lenguaje y alusiones literarias en la poesía de Francisco Brines: *Insistencias en Luzbel.*" *Hispania* 69.1 (1986): 1–11.

———. "Memory, Tradition and the Reader in the Poetry of Francisco Brines." *Modern Language Notes* 99 (1984): 308–26.

Bousoño, Carlos. "La poesía de Claudio Rodríguez." In Rodríguez, *Poesía 1953–1966,* 7–35. Madrid: Plaza y Janés, 1971.

———. "La poesía de José Angel Valente y el nuevo concepto de la originalidad." *Insula* 174 (1961): 1, 14.

———. *Poesía poscontemporánea. Cuatro estudios y una introducción.* Madrid: Jucar, 1985.

———. "Situación y características de la poesía de Francisco Brines." *Poesía 1960–1971: Ensayo de una despedida,* 11–94.

Bradford, Carole. "The Dialectic of Nothingness in the Poetry of Francisco Brines." *Taller Literario* 1.2 (1980): 1–12.

―――. "Francisco Brines and Claudio Rodríguez: Two Recent Approaches to Poetic Creation." *Crítica Hispánica* 2 (1980): 29–40.

―――. "Transcendent Reality in the Poetry of Claudio Rodríguez." *Journal of Spanish Studies—Twentieth Century* 7 (1979): 133–46.

Brines, Francisco. *Aún no.* Barcelona: Ocnos, 1971.

―――. *Las brasas.* Madrid: Ediciones Rialp, 1960.

―――. *Insistencias en Luzbel.* Madrid: Visor, 1977.

―――. *El otoño de las rosas.* Sevilla: Editorial Renacimiento, 1986.

―――. *Palabras a la oscuridad.* Madrid: Insula, 1966.

―――. *Poemas a D.K.* Sevilla: El mágico íntimo, 1986.

―――. *Poemas excluidos.* Sevilla: Editorial Renacimiento, 1985.

―――. *Poesía 1960–1971. Ensayo de una despedida.* Barcelona-Madrid: Plaza y Janés, 1974.

―――. *Poesía 1960–1977. Ensayo de una despedida.* Madrid: Visor, 1984.

―――. "Poética (Notas sobre poesía)." Molina 527–29.

―――. *El Santo inocente.* Madrid: Poesía para Todos, 1965.

―――. *Selección propia.* Madrid: Cátedra, 1984.

Cano, José Luis. *Poesía española contemporánea: las generaciones de posguerra.* Madrid: Guadarrama, 1974.

Cañas, Dionisio. "Introducción." *Francisco Brines. El rumor del tiempo* (Antología). Madrid: Mondadori, 1989.

―――. *Poesía y percepción (Francisco Brines, Claudio Rodríguez y José Angel Valente).* Madrid: Hiperión, 1984.

Cassell's Latin Dictionary. Edited by D. P. Simpson. New York: Macmillan, 1977.

Cirlot, J. E. *A Dictionary of Symbols.* Translated by Jack Sage. 2d ed. New York: Philosophical Library, 1971.

Colinas, Antonio. "Equilibrio de Francisco Brines." *Cuadernos Hispanoamericanos* 302 (1975): 479–81.

The Compact Edition of the Oxford English Dictionary. Oxford: Oxford University Press, 1971, 1979.

Corominas, Joan and Pascual, José A. *Diccionario crítico etimológico castellano e hispánico.* Madrid: Gredos, 1980.

Culler, Jonathan. *On Deconstruction. Theory and Criticism after Structuralism.* Ithaca: Cornell University Press, 1982.

Daydí-Tolson, Santiago. *Voces y ecos en la poesía de José Angel Valente.* Lincoln, Ne.: Society of Spanish and Spanish-American Studies, 1984.

Debicki, Andrew P. "Francisco Brines: Text and Reader." *Poetry of Discovery:* 20–39.

―――. "Intertextuality and Reader Response in the Poetry of José Angel Valente, 1967–1970." *Hispanic Review* 51 (1983): 251–67.

―――, ed. "Introduction: Critical Perspectives on Contemporary Spanish Poetry." Special Issue on Contemporary Spanish Poetry: 1939–1990. *Studies in Twentieth Century Literature* 16.1 (1992): 5–13.

―――. "José Angel Valente. Reading and Rereading." *Poetry of Discovery:* 102–22.

―――. "New Poets, New Works, New Approaches: Recent Spanish Poetry." *Siglo XX / 20th Century* 8 (1990–91): 41–53.

————. "Poesía española de la postmodernidad." *Anales de la Literatura Española* (Alicante) 6 (1988): 165–80.

————. "Una poesía de la postmodernidad: Los Novísimos." *Anales de la Literatura Española Contemporánea* 14 (1989): 33–50.

————. *Poetry of Discovery. The Spanish Generation of 1956–71.* Lexington: The University Press of Kentucky, 1982.

De Man, Paul. *Allegories of Reading: Figural Language in Rousseau, Nietzsche, Rilke, and Proust.* New Haven: Yale University Press, 1979.

————. "Semiology and Rhetoric." In *Textual Strategies. Perspectives in Post-Structuralist Criticism,* edited by Josué V. Harari, 121–40. Ithaca: Cornell University Press, 1979.

Derrida, Jacques. "Différance." *Margins of Philosophy.* Translated by Alan Bass. Chicago: The University of Chicago Press, 1982. [Originally "La 'Différance'" was an address presented before the Société française de philosophie, January 27, 1968, published in the *Bulletin de la Société Française de Philosophie* 62.3 July–September 1968: 73–101, Discussion: 101–120, and simultaneously in *Théorie d'ensemble,* coll. Tel Quel, Paris: Seuil, 1968. It subsequently appeared in *Marges de la philosophie.* Paris: Minuit, 1972. The original discussion of "Différance" is reproduced in *Derrida and Différance* 83–95.]

————. *Of Grammatology.* Translated by Gayatri Chakravorty Spivak. Baltimore: The Johns Hopkins University Press, 1976. [Originally *De la Grammatologie.* Paris: Minuit, 1967.]

————. *Positions.* Translated by Alan Bass. Chicago: The University of Chicago Press, 1981. [Originally *Positions.* Les Editions de Minuit, 1972.]

————. "Structure, Sign, and Play in the Discourse of the Human Sciences." *The Language of Criticism and the Sciences of Man: The Structuralist Controversy.* Edited by Richard Macksey and Eugenio Donato. Baltimore and London: The Johns Hopkins University Press, 1972. [Originally "La Structure, le signe et le jeu dans le discours des sciences humaines."]

————. *Writing and Difference.* Translated by Alan Bass. Chicago: The University of Chicago Press, 1978. [Originally *L'Ecriture et la difference.* Paris: Seuil, 1967.]

Derrida and Différance. Edited by David Wood and Robert Bernasconi. Evanston, Ill.: Northwestern University Press, 1988.

Díaz, Janet W. "Main Currents in 20th Century Spanish Poetry." *Romance Notes* 9 (1968): 194–200.

Diccionario de la Lengua Española. Real Academia Española. 19th ed. Madrid: Espasa-Calpe, 1970.

A Dictionary of Angels. Edited by Gustav Davidson. New York: The Free Press, 1967.

A Dictionary of the Bible. Edited by James Hastings. New York: Scribner's, 1906.

The Dictionary of Philosophy. Edited by Dagobert D. Eunes. 15 ed. Totowa, N.J.: Littlefield, Adams and Co., 1965.

"Encuentro con el 50. La voz poética de una generación." *Insula* 494 (1988).

Etymological Dictionary of Latin. Edited by T. G. Tucker. Chicago: Ares Publishers, 1931; reprinted, 1976.

García de la Concha, Víctor. *La poesía española de posguerra: teoría e historia de los movimientos.* Madrid: Ed. Prensa Española, 1973.

————. *La poesía española de 1935 a 1975.* 2 vols. Madrid: Cátedra, 1987.

García Hortelano, José Luis. *El grupo poético de los años 50*. Madrid: Taurus, 1970.

García Martín, José Luis. "La poesía completa de Francisco Brines." *Cuadernos Hispanoamericanos* 420 (June 1985): 194–200.

González Muela, Joaquín. *La nueva poesía española*. Madrid: Ed. Alcalá, 1973.

Grande, Félix. *Apuntes sobre poesía española de posguerra*. Madrid: Taurus, 1970.

Harper's Latin Dictionary. Edited by E. A. Andrews. New York: American Book Co., 1907.

Hart, Anita. "José Angel Valente: Poetry of Illumination and Unification." *Hispanófila* 105 (May 1992): 13–31.

———. "The Poet in José Angel Valente's Metapoetic Texts." *Hispanic Journal* 11.2 (Fall 1990): 119–36.

———. "The Poet, the Word and the Reader: José Angel Valente's Search for Poetic Expression," Ph. D. diss., Florida State University, 1986.

———. "Poetry and Language: Intertextuality in the Works of José Angel Valente." *Proceedings of the 1988 Florida State University Conference on Literature and Film* (1992).

Harvey, Irene E. *Derrida and the Economy of Différance*. Bloomington: Indiana University Press, 1986.

Hernández, Antonio, Ed. *Una promoción desheredada: la poética del 50*. Madrid: Zero-Zyx, 1978.

Jiménez, José Olivio. *Cinco poetas del tiempo*. Madrid: Insula, 1972.

———. "Claudio Rodríguez entre la luz y el canto: sobre 'El vuelo de la celebración.'" *Papeles de Son Armadans* 87 (1977): 103–24.

———. *Diez años de poesía española 1960–1970*. Madrid: Insula, 1972.

———. "Esplendor y apagamiento: una visión poética de la realidad." In *Francisco Brines. Antología poética*, 7–22. Madrid: Alianza, 1986.

———. "Fifty Years of Contemporary Spanish Poetry (1939–1989)." *Studies in Twentieth Century Literature* 16.1 (1992): 15–41.

———. "Hacia la verdad en *Alianza y condena* (1965) de Claudio Rodríquez." *Diez años de poesía española 1960–1970*: 145–74.

———. "Lucha, duda y fe en la palabra poética: a través de *La memoria y los signos (1966)*, de José Angel Valente." *Diez años de poesía española 1960–1970*: 223–42.

———. "Medio siglo de poesía española (1917–1967)." *Hispania* 50 (1967): 931–46.

———. "Poética y poesía de la joven generación española." *Hispania* 49 (1966): 195–205.

Johnson, Barbara. *The Critical Difference. Essays in the Contemporary Rhetoric of Reading*. Baltimore and London: The Johns Hopkins University Press, 1980.

———. "Translator's Introduction" to Jacques Derrida, *Dissemination*. Chicago: The University of Chicago Press, 1981.

Kerferd, G. B. "Logos." In *The Encyclopedia of Philosophy*, vol. 5, edited by Paul Edwards, 83–84. New York: Macmillan Publishing Co., rept. ed. 1972.

Lertora, Juan C. "'Poemas a Lázaro': Líneas de entrada a una poética." *Cuadernos Hispanoamericanos* 341 (1978): 393–400.

Mantero, Manuel. Ed. *Poesía española contemporánea. Estudio y antología*. Barcelona: Plaza y Janés, 1966.

Markus, R. A. "Illumination." In *The Encyclopedia of Philosophy*, vol. 4, edited by Paul Edwards, 129–30. New York: Macmillan Publishing Co., rept. ed. 1972.

Marra-López, José R. "Una nueva generación poética." *Insula* 221 (1965): 5.

———. "La poesía de José Angel Valente." *Insula* 219 (1965): 5.

Martínez Ruiz, Florencio, Ed. *La nueva poesía española: antología crítica: segunda generación de postguerra, 1955–1970.* Madrid: Biblioteca Nueva, 1971.

Martino, Florentino. "La poesía de José Angel Valente." *Papeles de Son Armadans* 51 (1968): 144–62.

Mas, Miguel. *La escritura material de José Angel Valente.* Madrid: Hiperión, 1986.

Mayhew, Jonathan. *Claudio Rodríguez and the Language of Poetic Vision.* Lewisburg, Pa.: Bucknell University Press, 1990.

Miller, J. Hillis. "Ariadne's Thread: Repetition and the Narrative Line." *Critical Inquiry* 3.1 (1976): 57–77.

———. "The Critic as Host." In *Deconstruction and Criticism,* edited by Harold Bloom et al., 217–53. New York: Continuum, 1979.

———. *The Linguistic Moment. From Wordsworth to Stevens.* Princeton: Princeton University Press, 1985.

———. "Stevens' Rock and Criticism as Cure." *Georgia Review* 30 (1976): 5–33 (part I) and 330–48 (part II).

Miller, Martha LaFollette. "Elementos metapoéticos en un poema de Claudio Rodríguez." *Explicación de Textos Literarios* 8 (1979–80): 20–23.

———. "Linguistic Skepticism in 'El vuelo de la celebración': A Counterpoint to Jorge Guillén's Linguistic Faith." *Anales de la Literatura Española Contemporánea* 6 (1981): 105–21.

Molina, Antonio. Ed. *Poesía española contemporánea: Antología 1939–1964: Poesía cotidiana.* Madrid: Alfaguara, 1966.

Moliner, María. *Diccionario de uso del español.* Madrid: Gredos, 1990.

Mudrovic, William. "Claudio Rodríguez's 'Alianza y condena': Technique, Development, and Unity." *Symposium* 33 (1979): 148–62.

———. "The Poetry of Claudio Rodríguez: Technique and Structure." Ph. D. diss., University of Kansas, 1976.

———. "The Progression of Distance in Claudio Rodríguez's *Conjuros.*" *Hispania* 63 (1980): 328–34.

———. "Time and Reality in Claudio Rodríguez's 'El vuelo de la celebración.'" *Anales de la Literatura Española Contemporánea* 6 (1981): 123–40.

Mundle, C. W. K. "Consciousness of Time." In *The Encyclopedia of Philosophy,* vol. 8, edited by Paul Edwards, 134–39. New York: Macmillan Publishing Co., rept. ed. 1972.

Nantell, Judith. "Francisco Brines's *Aún no*: Poetry as Knowledge." *Kentucky Romance Quarterly* 31.4 (1984): 413–24.

———. "Modos de ser en *Insistencias en Luzbel* de Francisco Brines." *Revista Canadiense de Estudios Hispánicos.* 12.1 (1987): 33–55.

———. "Retracing the Text: Francisco Brines's *Poemas excluidos.*" *Studies in Twentieth Century Literature* 13.2 (1989): 195–214.

———. "Writing and Reading: Dialectical Correlatives in Francisco Brines's *Insistencias en Luzbel.*" In *After the War: Essays on Recent Spanish Poetry,* edited by John Wilcox and Salvador Jiménez-Fajardo, 83–97. Boulder: Society of Spanish and Spanish-American Studies, 1988.

Nuñez, Antonio. "Encuentro con Claudio Rodríguez." *Insula* 234 (1966): 4.

Oxford Latin Dictionary. Edited by G. W. Glare. Oxford: Clarendon Press, 1982.

Persin, Margaret H. "José Angel Valente and The Anxiety of Influence." *Recent Spanish Poetry:* 26–44.

———. "Francisco Brines' *Insistencias en Luzbel:* Toward the Limits of Language and Being." *Recent Spanish Poetry:* 45–67.

———. "José Angel Valente: Poem as Process." *Taller Literario* 1.1 (1980): 24–41.

———. *Recent Spanish Poetry and the Role of the Reader.* Lewisburg, Pa.: Bucknell University Press, 1987.

———. "The Syntax of Assertion in the Poetry of Claudio Rodríguez." In *Recent Spanish Poetry:* 68–97.

Polo, Milagros. *José Angel Valente: Poesía y poemas* (Madrid: Narcea, 1983).

The Pre-Socratic Philosophers. Edited by G. S. Kirk and J. E. Raven. Cambridge: Cambridge University Press, 1957.

The Princeton Encyclopedia of Poetry and Poetics. Edited by Alex Preminger. Princeton: Princeton University Press, 1974.

Prieto de Paula, Angel L. "Claudio Rodríguez entre la iluminación y la muerte." *Insula* 444–45 (1988): 7, 8.

Quinn, Arthur. *Figures of Speech.* Salt Lake City, Utah: Gibbs M. Smith, 1982.

Quiñones, Fernando. *Ultimos rumbos en la poesía española.* Buenos Aires: Ed. Columba, 1966.

Ribes, Francisco. *Poesía última.* 3d ed. Madrid: Taurus, 1975.

Risco, Antonio. "Lázaro en la poesía de José Angel Valente." *Hispania* 56 (1973): 379–85.

Rodríguez, Claudio. *Conjuros.* Santander: Cantalapiedra, 1958.

———. *Desde mis poemas.* Madrid: Cátedra, 1984.

———. "Unas notas sobre poesía." Ribes 87–92.

Rodríguez Padrón, Jorge. "La poesía de José Angel Valente," *Cuadernos Hispanoamericanos* 222 (1968): 683–87.

Rubio, Fanny. "La poesía española en el marco cultural de los primeros años de posguerra." *Cuadernos Hispanoamericanos* 276 (1973): 441–67.

———. "Teoría y polémica en la poesía española de posguerra." *Cuadernos Hispanoamericanos* 361–62 (1980): 199–214.

Sala, José M. "Algunas notas sobre la poesía de Claudio Rodríguez." *Cuadernos Hispanoamericanos* 334 (1978): 125–41.

Sanz Echevarría, Alfonso. "La insistencia de Francisco Brines." *Jugar con fuego. Poesía y crítica.* [Avilés, Asturias] 3–4 (1977): 33–49.

Simón, César. "Algunos aspectos lingüísticos en la sátira de Francisco Brines." *Cuadernos de Filología* (June 1971): 63–70.

Sherno, Sylvia. "José Angel Valente: From the Dark Centre to the Limits." *Revista Canadiense de Estudios Hispánicos* 14.1 (Fall 1989): 161–73.

Silver, Philip. "New Spanish Poetry: The Rodríguez-Brines Generation." *Books Abroad* 42 (1968): 211–14.

Spivak, Gayatri Chakravorty. "Translator's Preface" to Jacques Derrida, *Of Grammatology.* Baltimore: The Johns Hopkins University Press, 1976.

Ugalde, Sharon. "José Angel Valente's *Material memoria* and the Poetic Process." *Pacific Coast Philology* 18 1.2 (1983): 52–58.

Valente, José Angel. "Conocimiento y comunicación." Ribes 155–61. Rpt. of "Conocimiento y comunicación." *Palabras a la tribu.* Madrid: Siglo Veintiuno de España Editores, 1971.

———. Interview. "José Angel Valente: un poeta en el tiempo." By Sol Alameda. *El País* 10 January 1988: 18–23.

———. Interview. "José Angel Valente y el 'punto cero' de la poesía." By Fanny Rubio. *El País* 14 December 1980: 6, 7.

———. *Poemas a Lázaro.* Madrid: Indice, 1960.

———. "Poética (Fragmentos de una poética)." Molina 489–90.

———. *Punto cero. (Poesía 1953–71).* Barcelona: Barral Editores, 1972.

Villar Ribot, Fidel. "La mirada del tiempo: En torno a *El otoño de las rosas* de Francisco Brines." *Hora de poesía* 51–52 (May-August 1987): 67–77.

Villena, Luis Antonio de. "De luz, de tiempo, de palabra, de hombres: sobre la poesía de Francisco Brines." *Insula* 338 (1975): 4–5.

———. "Sobre '*Insistencias en Luzbel*' y la poesía de Francisco Brines." *Papeles de Son Armadans* 89 (1978): 213–22.

Index